11+ Maths : 10 Minute Word Problem tests

By

A Henderson

Copyright Notice

Introduction

Internalising Math concepts is very important for a high Score.

It is easy to understand 11+ Math conceptually, after all it consists of mainly Key Stage 2 topics.

However, *under time pressure*, it is all too common to see students fumbling about with their formulae and their concepts, losing precious time.

What is needed is the ability to look at a problem, and have a *A-ha, I have seen it before*, moment.

And that is what the 11+ Winners do!

Most 11+ winners are so well conversant with the concepts that they don't have to spend too much time thinking about how to approach the problem, and which formulae to apply.

And how do they do this? With Practice, Practice and more Practice.

After you have gone through the theory, you should try to solve as many different problems as you can get your hand on, and this is where this book comes in!

This book contains 550 varied and interesting questions covering all important topics.

These questions are split into 55 tests with 10 questions in each test.

Each test should be done in 10 minutes.

Some Unique features of this book:

– Contains 500+ Word Problems covering ALL topics of 11+ Math.

– Problems split into bite sized chunks with 55 <u>Ten Minute</u> tests.

– All problems Fully explained with alternative methods for solving where applicable.

– Problems based around REAL 11+ Questions that have appeared in the recent past.

– Focus on the following important topics;

NUMBER SYSTEM

PERCENTAGE

PROFIT & LOSS

RATIO AND PROPORTION

FRACTIONS

FACTORS

STATISTICS

MEASURES

GEOMETRY

ALGEBRA

PROBABILITY

TEST 1

1. Pipe A can fill a tank in 4 hours. Pipe B can fill the same tank in 6 hours. If both pipes are open, how long will it take to fill the same empty tank?

   A   2.4 hrs   B   3 hrs   C   10 hrs   D   2 hrs

2. The arithmetic mean of 80 numbers is 55. If two numbers namely, 274 and 850 are removed, what is the arithmetic mean of the remaining numbers?

   A   36   B   68   C   42   D   51

3. Two racing cars; Mazda and Toyota, competed in a 10000 m long race. It took Mazda 40 minutes to reach the finish line while Toyota took 50 minutes. How far was Toyota from the finish line when Mazda reached the finish line?

   A   4000 m   B   2000 m   C   3550 m   D   3000 m

4. A man is 41 years old, and his son is 9. In how many years will the father be three times as old as his son?

   A   7 yrs   B   8 yrs   C   9 yrs   D   10 yrs

5. A man sold a book by mistake at 120% of the marked price instead of discounting the marked price by 20%. If he sold the book for £14.40, what should have been the correct selling price of the book?

   A   £12.30   B   £9.60   C   £8.40   D   £15.80

6. The show started at 13:45 and ended at 15:00. What is the time difference in seconds?

   A   4080 seconds   B   4500 seconds   C   5280 seconds   D   4140 seconds

7. The graph below shows the number of items sold on an online shop from 10 am to 2 pm.

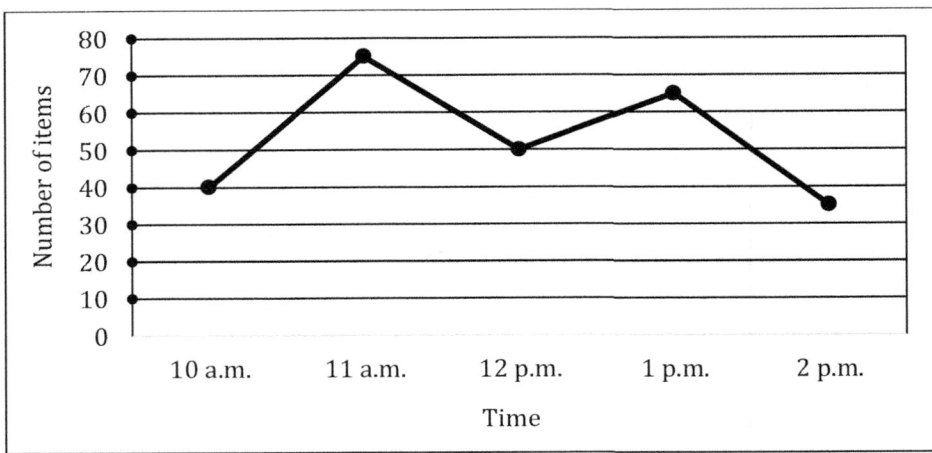

How many items were sold from 11 am to 1 pm?

A   190   B   150   C   170   D   130

8. A piggy bank has a total of eighteen notes of £50, fifteen notes of £20, and thirty notes of £10. How much money does the piggy bank have in total?

A   £1450   B   £1500   C   £1550   D   £1600

9. A farmer is planting tulips in his garden field. He plants 4 tulips in the first row, 8 tulips in the second row, 16 in the third row, 32 in the fourth row. If this pattern continues, how many tulips will the farmer plant in the tenth row?

A   1864   B   1024   C   512   D   2048

10. Tom owns a field which has irregular shape as shown below. What is its area?

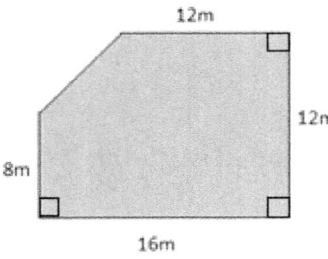

TEST 2

1. A data set of 9 numbers is given as follows: 15, 17, 9, 6, 19, 14, 11, 14, 21. If 14 is added to the list, which of the following will remain UNCHANGED?

   A   Only Mean   B   Only Median   C   Only Mode   D   All three

2. Harry owns a square field whose sides are 12 meters. There is a large square pit in the center of the field as shown below. What is the area of the field excluding the pit?

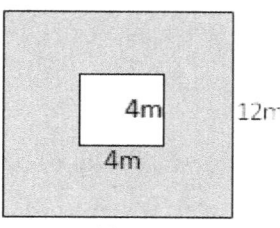

   A   120 m²   B   125 m²   C   128 m²   D   132.5 m²

3. What is the probability of getting two sixes when two six sided dice are rolled simultaneously?

   A $\frac{1}{6}$ B $\frac{1}{12}$ C $\frac{1}{36}$ D   1

4. Tommy is learning to classify fractions. He is given a fraction $\frac{69}{69}$; what kind of fraction is it?

   A   Improper   B   Proper   C   Mixed   D   Whole

5. A number is multiplied by two-thirds and the result is eight-elevenths. What is the number?

   A $\frac{16}{33}$ 　　　　 B $\frac{16}{23}$ 　　　　 C $\frac{12}{11}$ 　　　　 D $\frac{11}{12}$

6. At a party, two slices of pizza were left. One part was $\frac{3}{8}$ of a whole pizza and the other was $\frac{5}{12}$ of the whole pizza. Isaac wanted to get the larger portion. Which slice of pizza should he take?

   _____

7. If a particular piece of meat is added to $3\frac{4}{5}$ kg of an existing pile of meat, the total weight will be $8\frac{2}{3}$ kg. What is the weight of that particular piece of meat?

   A $\frac{72}{15}$ 　　　　 B $\frac{73}{25}$ 　　　　 C $\frac{73}{16}$ 　　　　 D $\frac{73}{15}$

8. The ratio of boys to girls in the class is 3 is to 4. Express 3 is to 4 as a percentage.

   _____

9. Michael gave his brother 30 marbles. If these were 50% of what he had, how many marbles did he have at first?

   A 　15 　　　　 B 　45 　　　　 C 　60 　　　　 D 　75

10. In a class, there are 24 boys and 32 girls. What is the ratio of girls to boys in the simplest form?

    A 　3:4 　　　　 B 　4:3 　　　　 C 　6:8 　　　　 D 　8:6

TEST 3

1. If it takes a carpenter 12 days to make 40 chairs, how long will it take him to make 500 chairs?

    A   150 days   B   160 days   C   200 days   D   250 days

2. The length and width of a rectangular lot are 24m by 18m. If the dimensions of the lot are increased by a factor of 1.5, what will be the new dimensions of the lot?

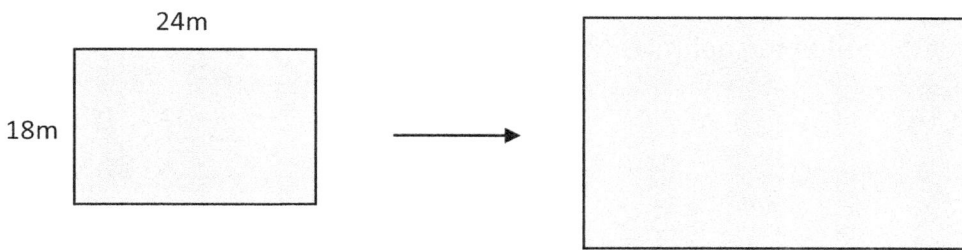

    A   16m x 12m   B   36m x 27m   C   25.5m x 19.5m   D   22.5m x 16.5m

3. Arvie is two years younger than twice the age of Jose. If Jose is 'J' years old, how old is Arvie?

    A   2-2J   B   2-J   C   2J-2   D   J-2

4. During a bet of numbers, I lost 58 from 85. After another bet, I won 15. What number do I have now?

    A   -12   B   12   C   42   D   -42

5. In a theater, there are 10 seats in the first row, 13 seats in the second row, 16 seats in the third row and so on. How many seats are there in the sixth row?

   A   19   B   22   C   25   D   28

6. The time it took to fill the tank with water was 4 hours 36 minutes and 24 seconds. How long would it take to fill the tank in seconds?

   A   16684sec   B   15684sec   C   15584sec   D   16584sec

7. Which of the following points is NOT on the x-axis?

   A $(0, 0)$ B $(9, 0)$ C $(0, 9)$ D $(1, 0)$

8. A bottle contains 750mL of water. There are 200 bottles of water in a box. How many liters of water is there in total?

   A   100L   B   150L   C   3.75L   D   1.5L

9. Jeremie is 149 cm tall. Rexell is 4cm taller than Jeremie. How tall is Rexell in meters?

   _____

10. The complement of an angle is twice the angle. What is the measure of the angle?

   A   15degrees   B   30degrees   C   45degrees   D   60degrees

TEST 4

1. Sara earned £15,423.80 during the lockdown. What place value does 5 represent?

   A   Thousands   B   Thousandths   C   Hundreds   D   Ten thousands

2. Which of the following numbers {-34, 2, 6, -3, -38, -87, -8} will be placed in the middle when arranged from lowest to highest?

   A   -3   B   6   C   2   D   -8

3. Immanuel has a probability of 0.92804156 on winning the game. What is the place value of the underlined digit?

   _____

4. The speed of light is 299,792,458 meters per second. Round-off the speed of light to the nearest hundred million.

   _____

5. Jacob estimated the height of a tree to be 5.645 meters. Anniel estimated the height of the same tree to be 5.695. If the actual height of the tree was 5.661, who was more accurate?

   _____

6. Which of the following points is farthest from the origin?

   A $(0, 0)$　　　　B $(0, 1)$　　　　C $(1, 0)$　　　　D $(1, 1)$

7. How many square tiles are there on a chess board if each row and column has 8 tiles?

   A 64　　　　B 16　　　　C 32　　　　D 24

8. One question of the test is to determine the lowest term of a fraction. Anna is having difficulty with the fraction $\frac{10}{15}$. What is the correct answer to the question?

   _____

9. What is the probability of drawing a red card from the deck of cards?

   A $\frac{13}{52}$　　　　B $\frac{1}{2}$　　　　C $\frac{1}{52}$　　　　D $\frac{39}{52}$

10. Shakira has answered $\frac{8}{15}$ of the questions. If she correctly answered half of them, what is her score in fractions?

   A $\frac{8}{7.5}$　　　　B $\frac{16}{15}$　　　　C $\frac{4}{15}$　　　　D $\frac{16}{30}$

TEST 5

1. Annie recycled $\frac{3}{4}$ pound of newspapers, $\frac{1}{2}$ pound of aluminum cans, and $\frac{7}{8}$ pound of clear glass. How many pounds of material did she recycle?

   A $\frac{16}{8}$ pounds   B $\frac{17}{8}$ pounds   C $\frac{18}{8}$ pounds   D $\frac{19}{8}$ pounds

2. Maria is playing with numbers. If she takes away the fraction $6\frac{3}{8}$ from a whole number 10, what fraction will she get?

   _____

3. Of the 300 workers of a vaccine factory, 40% are married. Convert 40% to fraction in lowest term.

   _____

4. In an 80-item test, Harvey answered 65% correctly. How many incorrect answers did he get?

   A 28   B 29   C 30   D 31

5. Find the value of 'x' if the volume of the shape is 30cm³

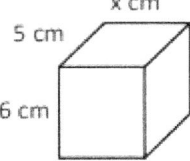

   _____

6. You can make seven sandwiches from a loaf of bread. How many sandwiches can be made from 12 loaves of bread?

    A   19   B 5   C 84   D 74

7. Sara is learning how to convert a statement in English into a mathematical expression. She easily gets the answer to the task "The sum of 35 and a number is divided by the same number". What would be the mathematical expression?

                                                             _____

8. Calculate the area of the shaded region shown below:

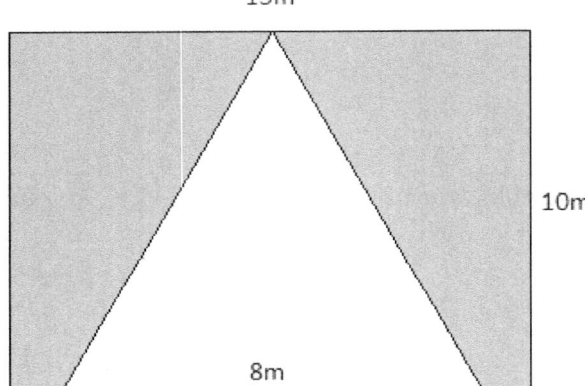

15m

10m

8m

9. John finishes the 100-meter race in 20 seconds. How long would it take him to run for 350 meters, if he runs at the same pace?

    A   2000 sec   B   700sec   C 70 sec   D 200sec

10. How many seconds are there in a single day?

    A   86400sec   B   1440sec   C   3600sec   D 76400sec

TEST 6

1. Jeremie wrote down a number between -23 and -20. Which of the following is a possible number that Jeremie has written?

   A   -19   B   -24   C   -22   D   -25

2. A particular newspaper has the policy of rounding off numbers to the nearest thousand for simplicity. If the actual number of participants in an event was 43,564, what would be the number of participants in that event as reported by the newspaper?

   A   40000   B   44000   C   43600   D   43560

3. Annie read the temperature on an old thermometer to be 24.45 degrees Celsius. Under same conditions, a digital thermometer having better accuracy, showed the temperature to be 24.5 degrees Celsius. What was the error made by the old thermometer?

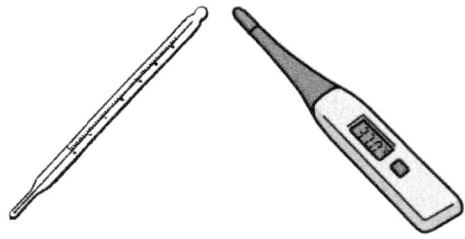

   A   0.5 ∘ C   B   0.05 ∘ C   C   1.5 ∘ C   D   1.05 ∘ C

4. What is the resultant number when two negative numbers; -4.5 and -4, are multiplied together?

   A   -18   B   18   C   -16   D   16

5. Sara is playing with numbers. She is thinking of the biggest 4-digit number that is divisible by 2, 3, 5, and 6. What is the possible value of that number?

   A   9900   B   10080   C   9990   D   9720

6. At a party, two slices of an extra-large pizza were left. One slice was $\frac{8}{9}$ of a medium pizza and the other was $\frac{6}{7}$ of a medium pizza. Harry chose the bigger slice. Which slice did he choose?

   _____

7. Mary is learning how to convert a statement in English into a mathematical expression. She easily gets the answer to the task "The difference of the squares of 22 and 55". What would be the mathematical expression?

   _____

8. Find the median of the following set of numbers: 7, 4, 5, 1, 1, 3, 4 ,6, 9, 2

   _____

9. A coin was tossed twice. What is the probability of getting a Heads both times?

   A   1%   B   25%   C   50%   D   75%

10. Mary bought a blouse and a skirt for £360. What was the price of the blouse if it cost 0.8 times the cost of the skirt?

   A   £200   B   £150   C   £160   D   £300

TEST 7

1. The total number of coins in a treasure chest is 12,045. Which of the following is the expanded form of 12,045?

    A 1×10,000+2×1,000+4×10+5   C 1×10,000+2×1,000+4×100+5
    B 1×10,000+2×1,000+4×1+5   D 1×1,000+2×1,000+ 4×100+5

2. A bag contains 10 red marbles, 5 yellow marbles, 3 green marbles, and 1 black marble. A marble is taken out from the bag randomly. What is the probability that this marble is a red marble?

    A $\frac{1}{19}$ B $\frac{10}{19}$ C $\frac{1}{20}$ D 1

3. Leo had 96 apples. He placed 12 apples in each plastic bag and sold each bag of apples for £24. How much did he get for selling the apples altogether?

    A £182   B £216   C £192   D £116

4. What is the least common multiple of the three prime numbers 3, 5, and 7?

    A 35   B 185   C 210   D 105

5. Jeremie listed several fractions with a common numerator 5. She arranged $\frac{5}{11}, \frac{5}{10}, \frac{5}{9}, \frac{5}{12}$ in ascending order. What would be the correct arrangement of these fractions in ascending order?

    _____

6. How would you express the fraction $\frac{1}{8}$ in percentage?

    A 1.25%   B 12.5%   C 25%   D 2.5%

7. A pie chart is shown below. What is the percentage area of blue portion, if the white portion makes 33% of the total area, green portion is $\frac{1}{4}$ of the total area, and the red and grey portions each have 17% of the total area?

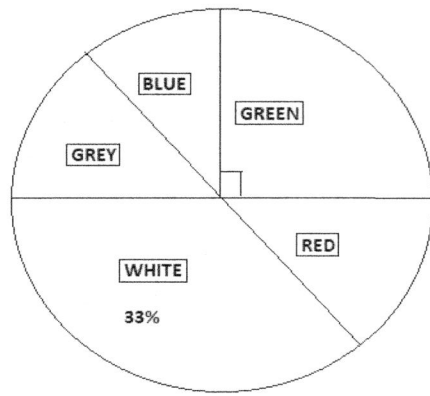

8. Mary is learning how to convert a statement in English into a mathematical expression. She struggles to get an answer to the task "If five is subtracted from three-fourths of a certain number, the result is 10". What would be the mathematical equation for this statement?

9. Jacob has a rectangular plot whose length is 3m less than four times the width. What is the dimension of the plot if the perimeter is 214 meters?

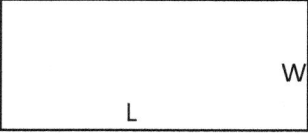

   A   85m x 22m   B   83m x 24m   C   90m x 17m   D   84m x 23m

10. George weighs 75kg while Harry weighs 76345g. How much heavier is Harry as compared to George?

   A   1.45 kg   B   2.345 kg   C   1.345 kg   D   76270 g

TEST 8

1. Jeremie weighs 39.52346 kilograms. What place value does 4 represent?

   A   Tenths   B   Hundredths   C   Thousandths   D   Ten thousandths

2. Maria is playing with numbers. She listed the factors of 1155. Which of the following is not a factor of 1155?

   A   11   B   5   C   7   D   13

3. Sam multiplied a number by itself three times (n x n x n) instead of squaring it (n x n). He got an answer of 64. What should have been the correct answer?

   A   16   B   24   C   32   D   4

4. A data set contains a total of 1000 whole numbers. The largest number is 11, the lowest number is 2, the average number is 5, and the number 6 occurred more than any other number in the data set. What is the mode of this data set?

   _____

5. Maria sewed 40 meters of cloth for dresses. If she used $\frac{5}{8}$ meters of cloth for each dress, how many dresses did she make?

   A   32   B   34   C   24   D   64

6. Mario is doing a math assignment on fractions. If a proper fraction $\left(\frac{2}{5}\right)$ is deducted from a mixed number $\left(3\frac{4}{7}\right)$, what should be the correct answer?

_____

7. Oliver is learning how to convert a statement in English into a mathematical expression. He easily gets the answer to the task "The square of the sum of 11 and 34". What would be the mathematical expression for this statement?

_____

8. A full deck of cards had a missing card. What is the probability of that missing card to be the King of Hearts?

A $\frac{1}{4}$ B $\frac{1}{52}$ C $\frac{1}{26}$ D 1

9. Find the volume of the three-dimensional rectangular block shown below:

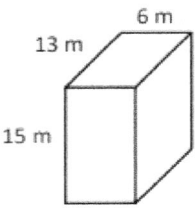

_____

10. Maria arranged some balls in such a way that the first row had 1 ball, second row had 2 balls, and the third row had 3 balls as shown below. What would be the total number of balls if there were a total of 5 rows?

A 10   B 15   C 20   D 25

TEST 9

1. Find the value of 'x' if the volume of the box shown below is 50m³.

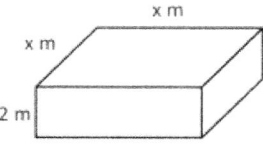

_____

2. A father owned 24,537 square meters of land. He equally distributed his land among his 3 children. How much land did each child get?

   A   8179 sqm   B   8177 sqm   C   8279 sqm   D   8178 sqm

3. What is the correct answer if Mary subtracts – 234 from – 954?

_____

4. Tom, Jacob, Harry, and Jeremie visited a mutual friend together on a particular day. Tom promised to visit him again every 6 days, Jacob every 5 days, Harry every 3 days and Jeremie every 2 days. After how many days will they again visit their friend together?

   A   24 days   B   30 days   C   36 days   D   45 days

5. Which of the following is an proper fraction?

   A $\frac{4}{4}$ B $\frac{3}{8}$ C $1\frac{2}{3}$ D   4

6. Williams bought 20 meters of cloth initially. He later bought an additional 50% of the cloth that he bought initially. How many meters of cloth did he buy in total?

   A   40m   B   10m   C   60m   D   30m

7. Anna is learning how to convert a statement in English into a mathematical expression. She easily gets the answer to the task "Twice a number increased by 5". What could be the possible mathematical expression for this statement?

   _____

8. 10 pancakes can be made from each box of flour. If there are 'n' boxes of flour, how many pancakes can be made?

   _____

9. James mixed 250mL of orange juice, 375mL of apple juice, 500mL of pineapple juice, and 400mL of mango juice in 1L of water. What is the total amount of concentrate that he made?

   A   2.525L   B   2.725L   C   1.525L   D   1.725L

10. What is the measure of the largest angle in a right-angled triangle?

   A   180degrees   B   100degrees   C   90degrees   D   60degrees

TEST 10

1. Maria jogged a distance of 5,371.32 meters. What distance did she jog in Kilometers? Give your answer correct to one decimal place

   _____

2. Michael had 144 jackets to sell. He managed to sell 9 dozen jackets. How many jackets did not sell?

   A   36   B   24   C   45   D   135

3. Jake received £51.67 from work. How much money would he have after buying a cake worth £12.36?

   A   £36.31   B   £39.31   C   £38.31   D   £29.31

4. Marie was grouping her earrings. Each time she grouped them by 4, 6 and 8, she found that she had 3 earrings remaining. When she grouped them by 5, there were no earrings left. What is the smallest possible number of earrings she had?

   A   27   B   50   C   24   D   75

5. Tom drinks $5\frac{1}{3}$ glasses of milk every day. How many glasses of milk does he drink in a week?

   A $37\frac{1}{3}$ B $35\frac{1}{3}$ C $5\frac{7}{3}$ D $37\frac{2}{3}$

6. A field is in the shape of a regular pentagon having sides of 5m. A fence is needed to be installed along the boundary of the field. How much would the fence cost in total if the cost of fence per meter is £25?
   (Note: All sides of a regular pentagon are equal)

   _____

7. A vase contains yellow and red flowers. What fraction of the flowers is yellow if the vase contains 9 yellow flowers and 15 red flowers?

   A $\frac{2}{8}$ B $\frac{3}{8}$ C $\frac{1}{8}$ D $\frac{1}{4}$

8. An apple weighs 100g while an orange weighs 80g. What is the total weight of 'a' apples and 'o' oranges?

   _____

9. A certain video on YouTube plays for 1 hour 13 minutes and 56 seconds. How long is it in seconds?

   A 4436 sec   B 4236 sec   C 4036 sec   D 4456 sec

10. The angles of a triangle are in the ratio 1:2:3 as shown in the figure below. What is the value of the largest angle?

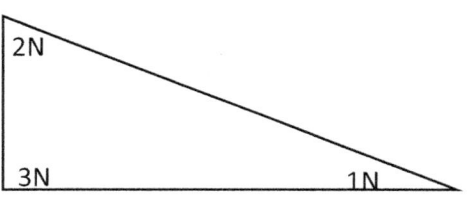

   A 120 degrees   B 60 degrees   C 180 degrees   D 90 degrees

TEST 11

1. The estimated value of π is 3.1415926. Determine the ten thousandths place.

   A   1   B   2   C   6   D   5

2. A data set of 6 numbers is as follows: 7, 3, 2, x, 1, 1
   Find the value of 'x' if the mean of the given data set is 2.5.

   _____

3. Find the total length of the fencing material needed to enclose a rectangular rose garden 85m by 15m?

   A   200m   B   150m   C   1275m   D   100m

4. What is the perimeter of a regular decagon in millimeters having sides of 2.35m?

   _____

5. How many $1\frac{1}{2}$ meter-ropes can be cut from $20\frac{3}{4}$ meter long rope?

   A   21   B   31   C   13   D   12

6. Emma's lantern is colored in red and blue. If $\frac{3}{11}$ of her lantern is red. What fractional part of the lantern is blue?

_____

7. Sara got 6 mistakes in a 50-question Math test. What percentage of her answers were correct?

   A   12%   B   44%   C   56%   D   88%

8. Kobe gave Jack and Rexell some playing cards. For every 3 cards given to Jack, 5 cards were given to Rexell. If a total of 48 cards were given to Jack and Rexell, How many more cards did Rexell receive than Jack?

   A   30   B   12   C   18   D   24

9. The scale on the map is 1cm:100km. What is the actual distance between two cities that are 3.25cm apart on the map?

   A   325km   B   0.0325km   C   3.25km   D   32.5km

10. Martin shuffles a full stack of playing cards and then picks up a card at random. What is the probability that Martin picks up a King?

   A $\frac{1}{52}$ B $\frac{1}{26}$ C $\frac{1}{13}$ D $\frac{1}{4}$

TEST 12

1. Harvey decided to write sixty-nine million, thirty-four thousand and thirty-five in standard form. Which of the following would give him the correct answer?

   A 69,340,035   B 69,034,035   C 69,304,350   D 69,034,350

2. Three friends bought different snacks. Harry bought a chocolate that cost £23, Harvey bought chips that cost £12, and Joseph bought a cake that cost £25. Who paid the price that represents the median value of the three prices?

   A Harry   B Harvey   C Joseph   D None

3. A candy costs £0.546, a chocolate costs £1.25, and a cookie costs £0.75. If I buy ten chocolates, one hundred cookies and one thousand candies, how much is the total cost?

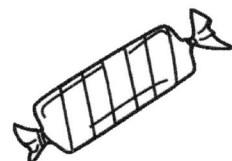  

   A £633.50   B £2.546   C £546   D £87.50

4. If the perimeter of a regular octagon is 20cm, what is its side length?

   A 20 cm   B 200 cm   C 2 cm   D 2.5 cm

5. What is the result if $7\frac{1}{2}$ is subtracted from $9\frac{1}{4}$?

   _____

6. There are 150 children playing in the park. If 40% of them are boys and the remaining are girls, how many girls are there?

   A   60   B   90   C   130   D   9

7. Shaira was able to sell 56 oranges. This was $\frac{4}{5}$ of the oranges she had originally. What is the ratio of the oranges sold to the original number of oranges?

   A   4:5   B   5:4   C   56:60   D   56:70

8. The google map has a scale of 1pixel: 4meters. If a certain rectangular lot was measured in the map and was 10 pixels by 20 pixels. What would be the area of the lot?

   A   800 sqm   B   1600 sqm   C   2400 sqm   D   3200 sqm

9. A banana costs £2 and an apple costs £3. If there are twice as many bananas as apples, how many bananas are there if the total cost of all fruits is £56?

   A   16 bananas   B   8 bananas   C   24 bananas   D   12 bananas

10. Three angles of a quadrilateral measure 25 degrees, 80 degrees, and 145 degrees. What is the measure of the fourth angle?

   A   100degrees   B   90 degrees   C   110degrees   D   40 degrees

TEST 13

1. In constructing a house, an engineer needed a total of 416,928 hollow blocks. How many blocks would the engineer need to order if they can only be bought in multiples of 10 thousand?

   _____

2. Jacob selected different numbers which were positive as well as negative. If he arranged them from least to greatest, what is the third highest number from the following numbers:
   {-65, 4, -12, -34, -6, -2}?

   A   -65   B   4   C   -12   D   -6

3. Jerry cleaned $\frac{2}{5}$ of the garden. What percent of the garden did he clean?

   _____

4. Jeremy bought 40 meters of cloth. He used 5% of it for pillowcases and 50% of it for bed covers. The remaining cloth was used for curtains. How many meters of cloth was used for curtains?

   A   22m   B   18m   C   25m   D   15m

5. Mary has candles in the shape of a cube having sides of 4cm. How many of those candles can fit in the box shown below?

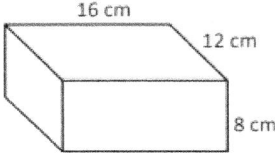

   _____

6. While browsing the newsfeed from Facebook, the 1000-pixel photo was viewed and enlarged by a scaling factor of 1.35. How many pixels were consumed by the photo?

   A   135 pixels   B   13500 pixels   C   135000 pixels   D   1350 pixels

7. There are a total of 1000 candies in the canteen. Fifty students entered the canteen and bought 'e' candies each. How many candies were left?

   _____

8. Marie decided to save money for her upcoming birthday. If she saves £1 on the first day, £2 on the second day, £4 on the third day and so on; how much money did she save after one week?

   A   £127   B   £63   C   £64   D   £32

9. A cake needs 0.25kg of sugar. How much sugar is needed in grams for 12 cakes?

   A   3kg   B   3000g   C   48kg   D   48000g

10. For every 25 meters, a tree is planted along the highway. If there are 135 trees, how long is the highway in kilometers?

   25m   25m   25m   25m

   A   160km   B   160m   C   3.375km   D   4km

TEST 14

1. Monique has £546,745 in her bank account. What is his balance rounded off to the nearest million?

   A   5 million   B   Zero million   C   One million   D   6 million

2. The radius of the earth is 6,371 km. Round off 6,371 to the nearest hundreds.

   _____

3. Jeremie has £1,00 and he decided to spend it on different foods. She bought twelve chocolates that cost £5 each, twenty candies that costs £1 each and a bottle of soda that cost £6.5. How much money was left?

   A   £13.5   B   £86.5   C   £60   D   £68.5

4. The total weight of 130 salt crystals is 6.5 g. What is the average weight of a salt crystal?

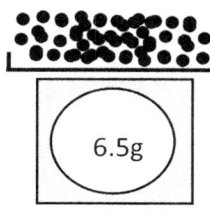

6.5g

   A   5g   B   0.5g   C   0.05g   D   0.005g

5. Two years from now, Tom's age will be a multiple of 8. His present age is not more than 72 and is a multiple of 9. What is his present age?

   A   36 years old   B   45 years old   C   54 years old   D   63 years old

6. Anniel is learning to classify fractions. He is given a fraction $\frac{12}{9}$. What kind of fraction is $\frac{12}{9}$?

   A   Improper   B   Proper   C   Mixed Number   D   Whole Number

7. What is the perimeter of a of a circle whose area is π^3?

   A π^3 B $2\pi^3$ C $2\pi^2$ D πr^2

8. An egg pie is divided into twenty equal parts. What percent is three parts of the whole egg pie?

_____

9. Marie, 1.6 meters tall, casts a shadow of 2.8 meters. If the tree casts a shadow of 4.2 meters, how high is the tree?

   A   2.8m   B   2.6m   C   3m   D   2.4m

10. Saira is learning how to convert a statement in English into a mathematical expression. She easily gets the answer to the task "The sum of a number and itself is subtracted by 100". What would be the answer?

_____

TEST 15

1. A water tank contains 234,567 liters of water. What digit is in the hundred-thousand place?

   _____

2. The four vertices of a square are located at (2, 2), (-2, 2), (2, -2), (-2, -2). Which of the following point is outside the square?

   A   Origin   B   (1, 1)   C   (2, -1)   D   (3, 0)

3. Jino has £500. After shopping, he had in his pocket £50 more than what he spent. How much was left in his packet?

   A   £225   B   £275   C   £325   D   £175

4. Martin is analyzing fractions. He wanted to know the Least Common Denominator (LCD) from the three random fractions. What is the LCD of $\frac{1}{3}, \frac{5}{9}, \frac{5}{6}$?

   A   3   B   6   C   9   D   18

5. Jermaine needs 3 meters of red ribbon, $\frac{4}{6}$ meter of pink ribbon, 2 meters of yellow ribbon, $\frac{3}{6}$ meter of brown ribbon and $2\frac{2}{6}$ meters of green ribbon. What is the total length of ribbon she needs?

   A $8\frac{1}{2}$m   B $7\frac{1}{2}$m   C   5m   D $9\frac{1}{2}$m

6. A one-meter green yarn was cut into two at 52 cm. What is the ratio of the smaller to longer piece?

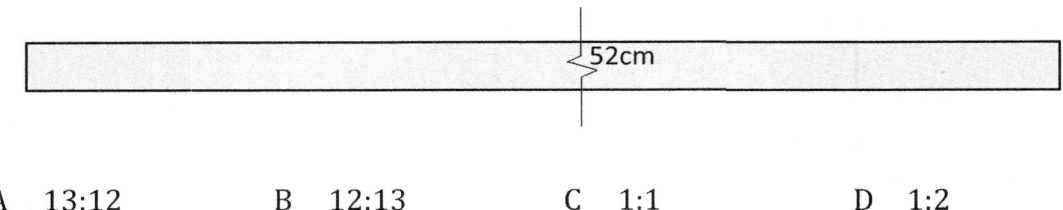

   A   13:12   B   12:13   C   1:1   D   1:2

7. Immanuel has N pounds. How much more is needed to have a total amount of £1000?

   _____

8. Emma is twice as old as Manny. Manny is 10 years old now. How old will Emma be two years from now?

   A   20 years old   B   18 years old   C   16 years old   D   22 years old

9. There are ducks and cows in a barn. The number of ducks is 10 less than thrice the number of cows. Each duck has two legs and each cow has 4 legs. If there are a total of 90 legs, how many ducks are there?

   A   11   B   12   C   23   D   24

10. It took Marcel 1 hour to walk 500m. If he walked for 1.5 hours at the same speed, how long did he walk in kilometers?

   A   0.75km   B   750m   C   75km   D   75m

TEST 16

1. Jeremie is investigating negative numbers. She writes the numbers between (-10) and (-15). What are the numbers between -10 and -15 that are arranged from least to greatest?

   _____

2. Anniel wants to write 12.5430 in words. What would be the correct answer?

   _____

3. Ann runs at a speed of 6.63 meters per second. If she runs for 12.4 seconds, what distance would she cover?

   A   81.212m   B   82.112m   C   82.312m   D   82.212m

4. The boy-scouts hike at $2\frac{1}{2}$ kilometers per hour. How far did they go after hiking for $2\frac{1}{2}$ hours?

   A $6\frac{1}{4}$km   B   5km   C $6\frac{1}{2}$km   D $5\frac{1}{2}$km

5. In December, an employee was given £15,750 of which 60% was his bonus. What was his wage?

   A   £9450   B   £25200   C   £6300   D   £26200

6. Maria has 49 yellow and 63 red beads. What is the least number of yellow and red beads that may be added so that the ratio of yellow to red beads will still be the same?

   A   6 yellow, 8 red   B   8 yellow, 6 red   C   7 yellow, 9 red   D   7 yellow, 7 red

7. 3 Apples were being sold for £5. Dominique bought 3 dozen apples. How much change did she receive if she gave £100 to the seller?

   A   £60   B   £80   C   £20   D   £40

8. The average of ten numbers is 7. If a certain number is removed, the average drops to 6. What is that number?

   A   20   B   14   C   10   D   5

9. Jacob weighed 47.24 kg. He gained 4,230 grams after one year. How much does he weigh now?

   A   51.47kg   B   89.54kg   C   51.40kg   D   51.44kg

10. There are five pieces of sawn lumber. Each piece is 6.25m long. What is the total length of the sawn lumber?

		6.25m		

   A   31.25m   B   30.25m   C   31.50m   D   31.75m

1. The mass of an object is 13.5342 grams. What place value does 2 represent?

_____

2. Jino has £103. He bought a ballpen for £8 and used the remaining balance to buy notebooks at £19 each. How many notebooks did he buy?

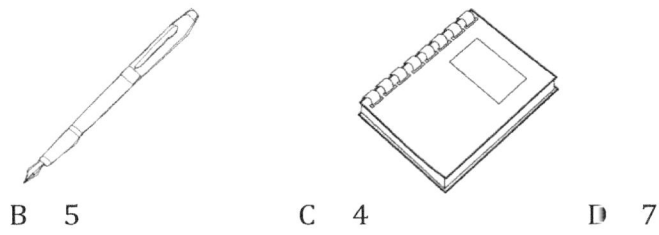

A   6   B   5   C   4   D   7

3. How many whole 100s are there in 36472?

_____

4. Arvie has £465.75 while Emmanuel has £524.15. How much more money does Emmanuel have as compared to Arvie?

A   £58.40   B   £44.60   C   £989.90   D   £979.90

5. Jeremie is investigating negative numbers. If she adds a negative number (-23.2) to a positive number (25.125), the result will be?

_____

6. The pie chart shown below represents different animals. What is the percentage of cats?

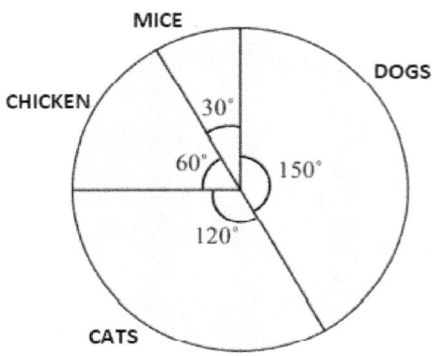

A   120%   B   33.33%   C   40%   D   50%

7. Sara is playing with numbers. She listed the factors of 30, 42, and 60. What is the greatest common factor of the three numbers mentioned above?

A   6   B   12   C   420   D   210

8. Jeremie is investigating negative numbers. What will be the result if she squares the negative number (-15)?

A   -225   B   -30   C   30   D   225

9. Marcel is analyzing fractions. He wants to make dissimilar fractions into similar fractions. The fractions are $\left\{\frac{1}{2}, \frac{2}{3}, \frac{4}{5}\right\}$. Write these as similar fractions.

_____

10. A famous sequence was introduced by Fibonacci wherein the next number is the sum of the previous two numbers {1, 1, 2, 3, 5, 8, …}. What is the 10th number in the sequence?

A   34   B   55   C   89   D   144

TEST 18

1. The length of the wire is 6.03456 meters. What is the value on the thousandths place?

   _____

2. A bacterium triples every hour. Initially, there are 10 bacteria. How many bacteria are there after 3 hours?

   A   90   B   180   C   270   D   540

3. Every ten minutes, a total of 125 apples are harvested. How many apples are harvested after one hour and 40 minutes?

   A   1250   B   12.5   C   12500   D   125000

4. Jeremie is investigating negative numbers. If she divides a positive number (135) by a negative number (-3), what would be the answer?

   _____

5. Rem is playing with numbers. She is counting by 18. What is the least multiple of 18 that is divisible by 27?

   A   36   B   54   C   108   D   144

6. The pie char shown below represents the number of students who play different sports in a college. Calculate the angle of the sector represented by baseball?

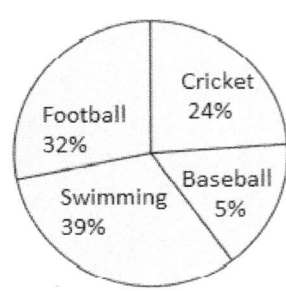

7. Manny bought $2\frac{1}{2}$ meters of cloth. He used $1\frac{3}{4}$ meters for the jacket. How many meters of cloth was left?

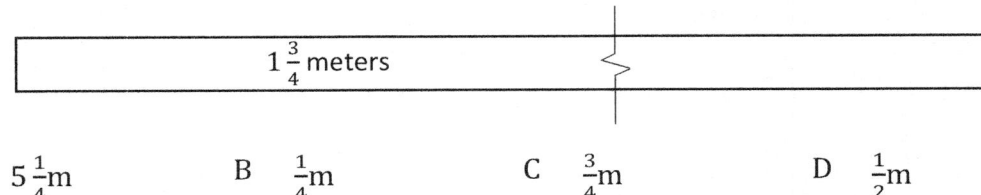

   A $5\frac{1}{4}$m   B $\frac{1}{4}$m   C $\frac{3}{4}$m   D $\frac{1}{2}$m

8. After giving his nephew 5% of her money, Anna now has £570. How much money did she have originally?

   A   £600   B   £598.50   C   £28.50   D   £541.50

9. Jake initially bought an equal number of apples and oranges. Later he bought an additional 20 oranges making the ratio of apples to oranges as 5:7. How many fruits did he buy altogether?

   A   50   B   70   C   120   D   60

10. Three girls gathered seashells on the seashore. Jeremie has twice as many seashells as Jerry. Jerry has $\frac{1}{3}$ as many as Jermaine. How many seashells did Jeremie gather if they have a total of 30 shells?

   A   10   B   15   C   5   D   20

TEST 19

1. Marie read the temperature on a digital thermometer as 22.195 degrees Celsius. What digit is on the hundredths place?

   _____

2. On a certain exam, a student gets 35 marks in Math. In science, he gets 21 marks more than he gets in math. In English he gets 12 marks less than he gets in science. How many marks does he get altogether?

   A   135   B   145   C   125   D   225

3. Amiel placed £100,000 in a bank. If the interest rate per year was 0.08 percent, what would be the amount of interest after one year?

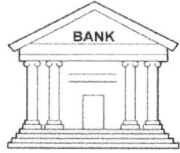

   A   £80000   B   £8000   C   £800   D   £80

4. The Venn Diagram below shows the number of students in a class who can speak certain languages.

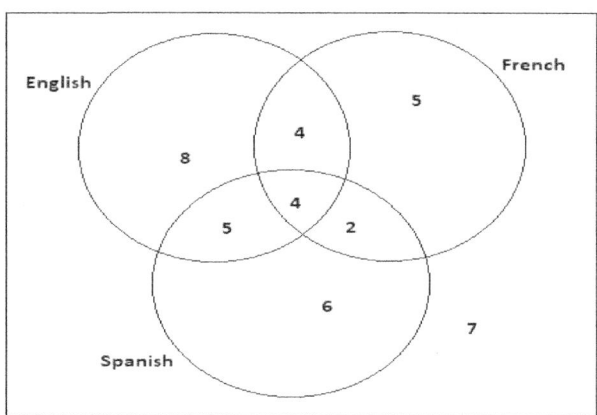

   How many students are there who speak ATLEAST 2 languages?

   _____

5. Refer to the Venn Diagram shown in Question 4. How many students do NOT speak English?

_____

6. Dominique is studying fractions. She reads a mathematical phrase "three out of fifty". How would this phrase be represented in standard mathematical form?

_____

7. Williams is analyzing fractions. There are four fractions under consideration. Three of them are equivalent to each other. Which one of the following fractions does not belong to the group?

A $\frac{3}{4}$ B $\frac{12}{16}$ C $\frac{20}{24}$ D $\frac{21}{28}$

8. Armel has £525 left in her wallet after shopping. The money she spent on shopping was 75% of her total money. How much money did she have initially?

A £131.25   B £656.25   C £2100   D £700

9. Twelve people can finish a job in 28 days. How many men are needed to finish the same job in 16 days?

A 21men   B 28men   C $\frac{48}{7}$men   D 7men

10. Anna likes to breed rabbits. Currently she has 55 rabbits. This is two less than thrice the number of rabbits she had last year. How many rabbits did she have last year?

A 57   B 19   C 25   D 27

TEST 20

1. Rexell has £13,749 in her bank account. She withdrew all of her money to the nearest hundred. How much money did she withdraw?

   A £10000   B £14000   C £13700   D £13750

2. Harry bought 7 pairs of shoes that cost £150 each. He sold them for an average price of £375. How much was his profit?

   A £5255   B £1575   C £1255   D £2350

3. Determine the value of $1000 \times 0.003 + 100 \times 0.06 + 10 \times 0.9$

   A 369   B 9.9   C 4.5   D 18

4. What is the smallest four-digit number that is divisible by 105?

   _____

5. Tom is analyzing fractions. He arranged similar fractions with different numerators from greatest to least. What should be the arrangement of $\frac{3}{9}, \frac{1}{9}, \frac{6}{9}, \frac{1}{3}$?

   _____

6. What is the median of the following data set: [1, 1, 1, 1, 2, 2, 2, 2, 3, 3, 3, 3, 4, 4, 4, 4]

   A   1   B   2   C   2.5   D   3

7. Maria celebrated her birthday. The ratio of men to women was 4:6. If there were 60 men, how many people attended her birthday?

   A   90   B   40   C   130   D   150

8. Marcel bought gifts worth £150. If he had 'J' pounds initially, how much money does he have now?

   _____

9. In a pageant, the number of votes Jake and Kobe got was in the ratio of 7:8. If there were 270 voters, how many voted for Kobe?

   A   126   B   136   C   144   D   154

10. Jeremie walks for 11minutes and 10 seconds going to the bus station. She waits for 3 minutes and 36 seconds before boarding the bus. From the station to the school, the bus travels for 15minutes and 14 seconds. What is the total time taken by her journey?

   A   1hr   B   0.5hr   C   1.5hr   D   2hr

1. On a certain day, the probability of raining is 0.35387453. Round-off the probability to the nearest thousandths place.

   _____

2. Sophia measured the amount of water collected by the water harvesting system to be 50L. If her error was +4L, what was the actual amount of water?

   A   46L   B   54L   C   52L   D   48L

3. A small juice box is 5cm by 7cm by 3cm. A carton of milk is 5cm by 10cm by 10cm. How much more liquid can the carton of milk contain?

   _____

4. If a number is multiplied by itself three times the result is 125, what is that number?

   A   -5   B   5   C   25   D   -25

5. Ben is analyzing fractions. He must convert a mixed number into an improper fraction. If he changes $2\frac{3}{4}$ into an improper fraction, what will be the answer?

   _____

6. A 10-meter bamboo strip is cut into two pieces. If one piece is $3\frac{6}{8}$ meters, how long is the other piece?

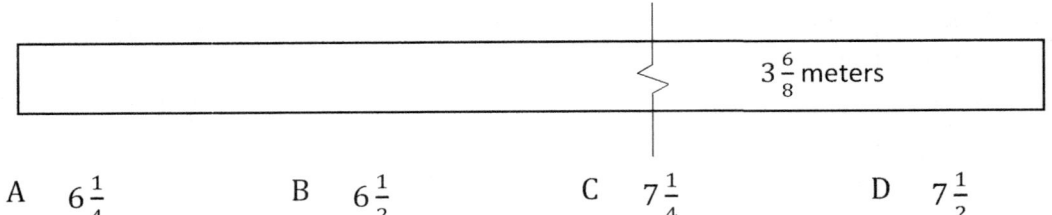

A $6\frac{1}{4}$ B $6\frac{1}{2}$ C $7\frac{1}{4}$ D $7\frac{1}{2}$

7. John answered correctly 21 out of 25 questions in the exam. What percent of his answers were wrong?

A 84%   B 16%   C 21%   D 25%

8. If 5 notebooks cost £156.75, what would be the cost of 20 notebooks?

A £783.75   B £39.1875   C £629   D £627

9. A 10-meter house casts a 6-meter-long shadow. If the tree beside the house casts a shadow of 3 meters, what is the height of that tree?

A 5m   B 4m   C 20m   D 15m

10. Shakira has £60 more than Jeremy, and the sum of their money is £300. How much money does Shakira have?

A £120   B £240   C £180   D £160

1. Immanuel measured the distance travelled by a car to be 25.294 km. If he was 0.23km short, what was the actual distance travelled?

   A   25.524km   B   25.064km   C   25.424km   D   25.544km

2. Jino bought 5 kilograms of sugar at £12 per kilogram. How much change did he receive if he gave two £50 notes to the shopkeeper?

   A   £60   B   £40   C   £50   D   £30

3. Find the angle 'y' if the three angles shown are on a straight line.

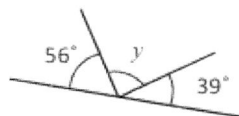

   _____

4. Jeremie is investigating negative numbers. If she multiplies a negative number (-5) three times by itself, what number will she get?

   A   -25   B   25   C   -125   D   125

5. Harry is analyzing fractions. If he multiplies a mixed number by another mixed number, he must change the mixed number first into an improper fraction before multiplying it. What would he get if he multiplies $5\frac{2}{3}$ by $2\frac{4}{5}$?

   _____

6. If a fraction $\left(\frac{7}{10}\right)$ is subtracted from $2\frac{1}{2}$ and the result then added to $\frac{4}{5}$, what would be the result?

_____

7. John's bank balance is 5% more than what it was 3 years ago. Currently his bank balance is £150,750. What was his bank balance 3 years ago?

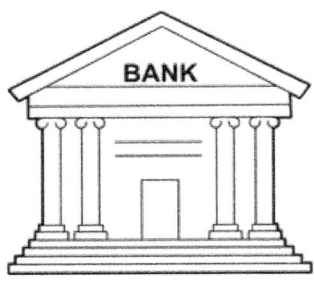

A   £143571.42   B   £158287.50   C   £160000   D   £15000

8. On the table, there are 20 ballpens consisting of black and red colors. Which of the following cannot be a possible ratio of black to red ballpen?

A   1:2   B   1:1   C   2:3   D   2:8

9. A sachet of juice powder is mixed in 8 glasses of water. How many sachets of juice powder are needed to be mixed in 48 glasses of water?

A   6   B   12   C   384   D   8

10. Saira weighs 5 kilograms more than Shaira. Their combined weight is 41 kilograms. What is the weight of Saira?

A   18   B   23   C   36   D   24

TEST 23

1. John received £50 from Harry, £100 from Harvey, £125 from Emmanuel and £75 from Anniel on his birthday. How many £50 jackets can he buy from this money?

   A   5   B   6   C   7   D   8

2. How many $100 bills are there in $125000?

   A   1250   B   125   C   12500   D   12.5

3. A piece of land has a perimeter of 6542.13 feet. What is its perimeter in yards if each yard is three feet long?

   A   2180.71 yds   B   19626.39 yds   C   2180.61 yds   D   19526.39 yds

4. Jason is solving a question which involves multiple mathematical operations. What correct answer will he get from the expression -2.5×4 - 12÷3?

   _____

5. Rem is playing with numbers. What is the LCM of two numbers if their HCF is 6 and their product is 1296?

   A   216   B   432   C   864   D   108

6. Anniel is learning to classify fractions. If he is given a fraction $4\frac{2}{3}$, what kind of fraction is it?

A   Improper   B   Proper   C   Mixed Number   D   Whole Number

7. Jeremy runs at a speed of $\frac{31}{4}$ meters per second. If she ran for 50 seconds, how many meters did she run?

A $385\frac{1}{2}$m   B $387\frac{1}{2}$m   C $387\frac{1}{4}$m   D $386\frac{1}{2}$m

8. Sara is analyzing fractions. She wanted to know the number midway between fractions. What fraction is midway between $\frac{2}{3}$ and $\frac{4}{5}$?

_____

9. Mario harvested 40 kilograms of apples. He kept $10\frac{3}{5}$ kilograms for himself and gave the rest to his relatives. How many kilograms of apples did he give?

A $29\frac{2}{5}$kg   B $29\frac{3}{5}$kg   C $30\frac{3}{5}$kg   D $30\frac{2}{5}$kg

10. The angles of the triangle shown below are x, 3x-2, and 50-x. What is the measure of the smallest angle?

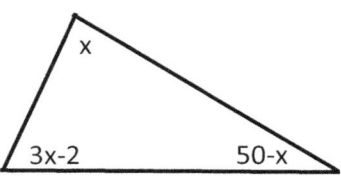

A   44 degrees   B   130 degrees   C   6 degrees   D   4 degrees

TEST 24

1. Jason bought 6 dozen of assorted size jackets at £300 a dozen. He sold them at the rate of 3 jackets for £100. How much money did he gain?

   A £2400   B £200   C £600   D £240

2. Sophie can type 30 words per minute. How long would she take to type 3423 words?

   A 102690 min   B 114.1 min   C 92690 min   D 115.1 min

3. The amount of water in a tank was decreasing at a rate of 5mL/min. Initially, the tank contained 100mL. How much water would remain after 5 minutes?

   A 75mL   B 25mL   C 95mL   D 50mL

4. How many slices of pizza are there in 5 pizzas if each slice is $\frac{1}{8}$ of a pizza?

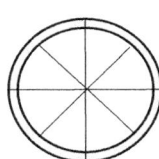

   A 13   B 20   C 40   D 80

5. Jack is analyzing fractions with similar numerators but different denominators. If he picked the smallest fraction among $\left\{\frac{2}{10}, \frac{2}{11}, \frac{2}{9}, \frac{2}{7}\right\}$, what fraction would it be?

   _____

6. Jacob wrote three fractions randomly. Out of curiosity, he adds the fractions $\left\{\frac{4}{6}, \frac{6}{8}, \frac{8}{10}\right\}$. What will be the result?

_____

7. 15 boys and 25 girls attended a party. What percent of the group was girls?

   A   62.5%   B   37.5%   C   166.67%   D   60%

8. A manager receives a basic monthly pay of £10,000 plus a cost-of-living allowance which is 15% of his basic pay. What is his total monthly income?

   A   £1500   B   £150   C   £15000   D   £11500

9. A coin is tossed followed by a dice. Find the probability of getting a head on the coin and a six on the dice.

   A $\frac{1}{4}$ B $\frac{1}{2}$ C $\frac{1}{6}$ D $\frac{1}{12}$

10. Jack planted 3 more than half of what Rexell had planted. Altogether, they planted 21 trees. How many plants did Jack plant?

   A   18   B   12   C   6   D   9

TEST 25

1. By mistake, Ann multiplied a number by 9 instead of dividing it by 9. She got 405 as the answer. What should have been the correct answer?

    A   45   B   5   C   9   D   81

2. Jerry bought a uniform that cost £250.50. If he sold it for £351.85, how much would be his profit?

    A   £101.35   B   £602.35   C   £102.35   D   £601.35

3. Anne has a cubical - shaped tank. If each side has a length of 2 meters, what is the volume of the tank?

    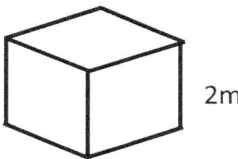

    A   8 cu.m   B   4 cu.m   C   16 cu.m   D   12 cu.m

4. Mario is analyzing fractions. He is converting a mixed number into an improper fraction. What fraction will he get if he converts $3\frac{5}{7}$ into an improper fraction?

    _____

5. Dominique is studying decimals. What fraction will she get from the decimal number 0.125?

    _____

6. A class consisted of 50 students. On a particular day, only 35 were present due to bad weather. What is the ratio of the number of absentees to the number of students who are present?

   A   7:3   B   3:7   C   7:10   D   10:7

7. Ivet and Harvey received chocolates in the ratio 3:5 respectively. If Harvey received 45 chocolates, how many chocolates were given to both of them together?

   A   27   B   72   C   27   D   18

8. Martin is 65kg. He gained 'x' grams during vacation. What is his new weight now?

   _____

9. If the numerator and denominator of a fraction is increased by 'n' and 'd' respectively, what would be the new fraction if the original fraction was $\frac{8}{15}$?

   _____

10. Anne is making a bracelet made of beads of different colors. The number of blue beads is three more than twice the number of red beads. If a bracelet has a total of 30 beads, how many blue beads are there in a single bracelet?

    A   27   B   21   C   18   D   19

TEST 26

1. What is the length of each equal side of a pentagonal field with a perimeter of 200meters?

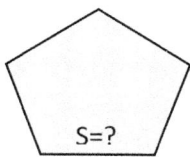

S=?

A   50m   B   40m   C   25m   D   20m

2. Rem is playing with numbers. She listed the prime factorization of 462. Breakdown 462 in its prime factorization.

_____

3. What would be the difference in the area of two squares if the sides of the squares are 4m and 5m respectively?

A   9 sq.m   B   1 sq.m   C   81sq.m   D   41 sq.m

4. Dominique converts an improper fraction to a mixed number. What answer will she get if she converts $\frac{24}{7}$ into a mixed number?

_____

5. Harry is analyzing fractions. He multiplied three fractions with each other and observed the result. What is $\frac{3}{4}$ of $\frac{4}{5}$ of $\frac{5}{6}$?

A $\frac{1}{2}$ B $\frac{1}{3}$ C $\frac{1}{4}$ D $\frac{2}{3}$

6. Jacob is investigating what fraction will be equivalent to itself. Which of the following is equivalent to $\frac{6}{18}$?

    A $\frac{2}{7}$ B $\frac{1}{3}$ C $\frac{3}{10}$ D $\frac{2}{9}$

7. Three similar fractions are added to each other. What would be the result if $\frac{1}{4}, \frac{3}{4}, \frac{8}{4}$ are added together?

    _____

8. In a class of 32 pupils, 20 are girls. What is the ratio of boys to girls?

    A 3:5   B 5:3   C 5:8   D 3:8

9. A tailor sews 6 dresses in a day. How many days will it take her to sew 3 dozen of dresses?

    A 2 days   B 9 days   C 5 days   D 6 days

10. A person needs 8 glasses of water every day. How many glasses of water are needed by twenty nine people in three days?

    A 290   B 240   C 232   D 696

1. A triangle has sides measuring 12m, 18m and 15m. What is its perimeter?

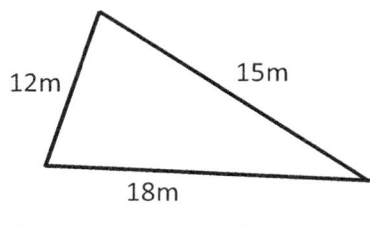

  A 180m   B 45m   C 3m   D 90m

2. Jacob selected two numbers from one to nine. The selected numbers were 3 and 6. He combined them to form a single number '36' and broke it down into its prime factors. What are the prime factors of 36?

                          _____

3. How much is a kilogram of meat if Monique bought $\frac{1}{4}$ kilogram of meat for £17.75?

  A £71   B £51   C £80   D £68

4. Harry is solving fractions based on the mathematical statement "three-fifths less than three-fourths" He doesn't know if the value is a positive fraction or a negative fraction. What could be the correct answer?

                          _____

5. The ratio of goats to cows in the farm is 1:3. Express this as a fraction.

                          _____

6. A football team lost 20% of the games played in the tournament, and won all the games that they did not lose. If they played 20 games, how many games did the team win?

   A   16   B   25   C   4   D   5

7. The lay-out of a lot is 10m by 12m. Each dimension is increased by 50%. What is the ratio of the original area to the new area?

   10m [rectangle] → [larger rectangle]

   12m

   A   1:4   B   4:1   C   4:9   D   9:4

8. Mary bought 15 sacks of rice for £12,300. How much is the cost of a sack of rice?

   A   £184500   B   £185500   C   £830   D   £820

9. Mary is going to give money to each of her three children for their allowance in the ratio 9:6:3. How much is the biggest share if the smallest share is £150?

   A   £150   B   £300   C   £450   D   £600

10. If you take out 5 from thrice the number of lemons that Tom had in the beginning, the result is 25. What was the original number of lemons that Tom had?

   A   10   B   20   C   30   D   25

TEST 28

1. What is the perimeter of an octagon whose equal sides measure 9m each?

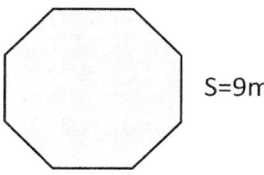 S=9m

   A 720m   B 72m   C 81m   D 90m

2. Find the sum of all multiples of 4 between 10 and 30.

   A 100   B 40   C 60   D 80

3. Harry is analyzing fractions. He is learning how to change an improper fraction into a mixed number. What will be the answer if $\frac{20}{3}$ is changed into a mixed number?

                                                    _____

4. How many $\frac{5}{6}$ are there in the whole number 50?

   A $41\frac{2}{3}$ B $41\frac{1}{3}$ C 60   D 40

5. Jacob is learning how to subtract a fraction from a whole number. What will be the result if he subtracts $\frac{7}{12}$ from 5?

                                                    _____

6. Five sixths of the total number of candidates passed the board exam. What percent of candidates failed?

   A 83.33%   B 66.67%   C 33.33%   D 16.67%

7. Due to bad weather, only 20 out of 60 people attended the meeting. What percent of the group attended?

   A 83.33%   B 66.67%   C 33.33%   D 16.67%

8. Ann has green and yellow beads in her drawer. The ratio of green to yellow is 3:8. If there are 21 green beads, how many beads are there in total?

   A 56   B 35   C 77   D 48

9. Jacob has a nephew and a niece. His nephew is $\frac{5}{7}$ times as old as his niece. His niece is 18 months older than the nephew. How old is his niece in months?

   A 45 months   B 63 months   C 72 months   D 54 months

10. A strawberry weighs 40g while a grape weighs 35g. What is the difference between the total weights of 's' strawberries and 'g' grapes?

                                                _____

1. At a rate of £180 per hour, how much will Shakira earn from Monday to Saturday if she works 5 hours a day?

    A   £5400   B   £900   C   £1800   D   £3600

2. Jacob is trying to round off the number 96 to the nearest multiple of ten. What would be the correct answer?

    A   90   B   100   C   110   D   80

3. Harry is analyzing fractions. The reciprocal of a number is one divided by that number. What is the reciprocal of $4\frac{1}{3}$?

    _____

4. Mangoes are sold at the rate of £12 per kilogram. What is the cost of $10\frac{1}{2}$ kg of mangoes?

    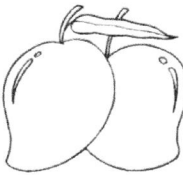

    A $22\frac{1}{2}$kg   B   126kg   C $120\frac{1}{2}$kg   D   £126

5. Jacob is learning how to carry out subtraction on mixed numbers. What answer will he get if the question is $10\frac{2}{3}$ less than $20\frac{4}{5}$?

    _____

6. Sara has 35 pieces of beads. If she gave 20% to her friend, how many beads were left?

   A   28   B   7   C   21   D   14

7. Maria correctly answered two more than thrice her wrong answers in a 26-item test. What is the ratio of her wrong answers to correct answers?

   A   10:3   B   3:10   C   3:13   D   10:13

8. If apples and mangoes are in the ratio 30:5, and mangoes and oranges are in the ratio 12:3, then how many oranges would there be for 168 apples?

   A   7   B   24   C   18   D   36

9. Monique and Yves were given 432 candies by their friend in the ratio 5:7. How many more candies did Yves get compared to Monique?

   A   252   B   180   C   72   D   144

10. A right triangle has sides in the ratio 3:4:5. If the hypotenuse (the longest side) has a length of 25, what would be the other dimensions of the triangle?

25

   A   15 and 20   B   10 and 15 C   15 and 25   D   10 and 25

TEST 30

1. Jacob is trying to get the multiple of 8 nearest that is closest to a certain number. What is the multiple of 8 closest to 2345?

   A   2360   B   2352   C   2344   D   2350

2. Jacob is trying to multiply fractions. What will he get if he multiplies three-fifths and three-fourths with each other?

   _____

3. Yves is analyzing fractions. He subtracts two fractions from each other but does not know if the answer is a positive nor a negative fraction. What is the correct answer if $15\frac{1}{4}$ is diminished by $5\frac{1}{2}$?

   _____

4. Emmanuel harvested 400 mangoes. He gave 5% of the mangoes to his neighbor. His family ate 10% of the remaining mangoes. How many mangoes are left?

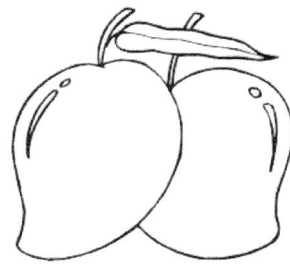

   A   342   B   380   C   242   D   200

5. In a class of 80 pupils, there are 52 girls and the remaining pupils are boys. What percent of the whole class is boys?

   A   35%   B   65%   C   30%   D   70%

6. Anne has £210 and Annie has 80% of what Anne has. How much money do they have together?

   A   £168   B   £100   C   £378   D   £42

7. 5 out of 8 students in the school are girls, and the remaining students are boys. If the school has 192 students, how many are boys?

   A   36   B   45   C   64   D   72

8. A tree was cut into 3 pieces whose lengths were in the ratio 3:4:5. If the longest piece was 20 feet. How tall was the tree?

   A   40m   B   48m   C   240m   D   28m

9. If apples and mangoes are in the ratio 15:8, and mangoes and oranges are in the ratio 12:4, then what is the ratio of apples to oranges?

   A   45:8   B   5:3   C   6:13   D   8:45

10. A right triangle has sides in the ratio of 5:12:13. If the smallest side has a length of 10 meters, what will be the perimeter of the triangle?

   A   50m   B   40m   C   60m   D   55m

1. Amy has 63 cm of ribbon. She used one-third of it on her project. Her mother then gave her another 10 cm of ribbon. Find the total length of ribbon Amy has now.

   A   42 cm   B   62 cm   C   52 cm   D   32 cm

2. Daniel is 149.17 cm tall, while James is 60 inches tall. Who is taller between the two?
   (Note: 1 inch = 2.54 cm)

   _____

3. Betty bought 8 boxes of colored pens and paid £52.00. She has 56 colored pens in total. How much does each box cost and how many pens are there in each box?

   _____

   _____

4. If -4 is substituted for x in the expression $-4x + 2x - kx - 20$, the result is 0. Find the value of k.

   A   3   B   22   C   8   D   15

5. A class consists of 56 students. 32 of them are girls while the rest are boys. What is the ratio of the number of boys to the number of girls in the class?

   A   4:3   B   3:4   C   4:7   D   7:4

6. Jeremy carries a Mathematics book that weighs 0.135 kg. Determine the weight Jeremy carries if he carries 10 books with an average weight of 0.135 kg.

_____

7. There are 90 girls and 72 boys in a school fair. The coordinator would like to arrange all the students in equal rows with only girls or boys in each row. What is the greatest number of students that can be in each row?

   A   36   B   18   C   24   D   9

8. Sara loves to write scripts. She can write two pages every $\frac{1}{12}$ hour. How many pages can she write in a span of 30 minutes?

   A   10 pages   B   11 pages   C   12 pages   D   15 pages

9. A box of vegetables weighs 13.021 kg. Calculate the weight of 50 boxes of vegetables.

_____

10. Thomas recorded the time he takes to walk from home to four different landmarks near his house as shown in the table below.

Landmark	Time
Park	10.6 min
School	10.16 min
Market	10.62 min
Candy Store	10.66 min

Determine which landmark is nearest to his house.

   A   Park   B   Market   C   School   D   Candy Store

TEST 32

1. Miguel spends 183.765 minutes playing video games. Round off the time to the nearest hundredths.

    A   184 minutes   B   183.7 minutes   C   183.77 minutes   D   200 minutes

2. A car travels from City A to City B. It leaves City A at 6:30 AM and reached City B at 10:45 PM. How long did the car travel for?

    A   15 hours and 15 minutes   C   20 hours and 30 minutes

    B   16 hours and 45 minutes   D   16 hours and 15 minutes

3. The length of a rectangle is 5 more than its width. Its perimeter is 60 cm. Find its length and width.

    L = ?   W = ?

    W = _____ cm

    L = _____ cm

4. Country X has a population of 93, 276, 810. What is the place value of 9 in the number 93, 276, 810?

    A   thousands   B   ten millions   C   millions   D   hundred thousands

5. A rectangular box has dimensions of 6 inches by 4 inches by 27 inches. A second rectangular box has a volume twice of the first and has a base 9 inches by 6 inches. Determine the height of the second box.

    A   25 in   B   22 in   C   24 in   D   27 N

6. Mary has a 4-digit number written on her paper. The digits are 1, 9, 4, and 6. When rounded to the nearest hundreds, her number is 4900. What is the number on Mary's paper?

_____

7. Matt plans to study all his subjects. If he allots $\frac{1}{5}$ of an hour to review his notes on each subject, how much time does he need to review all 8 subjects?

A $1\frac{3}{5}$ hours   B $1\frac{1}{6}$ hours   C $\frac{9}{5}$ hours   D $1\frac{2}{5}$ hours

8. The price of a book is **£b**. The bookstore has a promo sale, and all the books are 25% off. You have a voucher that will give you £2 discount on your total purchase. If you buy 6 books, how much will you need to pay?

_____

9. If you pour water into a tank at a rate of 25 liters per minute, at what rate is the tank being filled in kiloliters per hour?

_____

10. The sum of the two angles of a triangle is four times the third angle. What is the sum of the first two angles?

_____

1. Jenny loves to collect pictures. When rounded to the nearest thousand, the number of pictures she collected is 2000. What might be the actual number of pictures that she has?

   A   2531   B   2912   C   1487   D   1759

2. Cara and Miguel both bought groceries today. Cara buys groceries every 8 days and Miguel buys every 12 days. How many days will it be until Cara and Miguel buy groceries on the same day again?

   _____

3. I am a three-digit number. All my digits are different. My tens digit is less than 5. My ones digit is greater than my hundreds digit. I am divisible by 3 and 7. What number can I possible be?

   A   546   B   525   C   435   D   315

4. Sarah needs to deliver 18 cookies, 12 brownies, and 24 cupcakes. She can pack only one type of pastry in each box, and she must pack the same number of pastries in each box. What is the greatest number of pastries Sarah can pack in each box?

   A   12   B   9   C   8   D   6

5. Ed is renovating his house and needs more wood for shelving. He needs 245 planks of wood, but they only come in packs of 10. If each pack costs £8.99, how much will he need to spend?

   _____

6. Mika can type 1216 words every 8 minutes. How many words can she type in 1.45 hours?

  A   13224   B   13244   C   12344   D   13324

7. Jade collects shells. Every day, she collects 6 shells. On every fourth day, she gives 4 shells to her friend. If Jade started with 24 shells, on which day will she have exactly 70 shells?

  A   10th day   B   12th day   C   7th day   D   9th day

8. A wire 60 cm in length is cut into two parts in the ratio 2:1. Each part is bent to form a square. What is the total area of the two squares?

  A   162 cm^2 B   125 cm^2 C   130 cm^2 D   147 cm^2

9. Bryce wants to install 3 by 3 sq.cm tiles in his room. If his rectangular room has dimensions 9 cm by 10 cm, how many tiles will he need to cover his whole room?

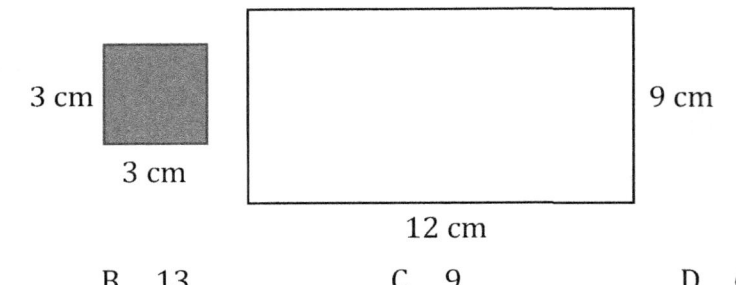

  A   12   B   13   C   9   D   6

10. A smartphone costs £136.90. As time goes on, its value goes down by £5.50 per year. What is the value of the smartphone after 6 years?

  A   £109.40   B   £103.90   C   £110.50   D   £105.50

TEST 34

1. Two numbers have 3 and 84 as their HCF and LCM, respectively. If the sum of the two numbers is 33, then which of the following could be one of the two numbers?

   A   15   B   21   C   48   D   84

2. Matt works in a shop and earns £12.40 every week. How much will he earn in 25 weeks?

   A   £3100   B   £310   C   £30.10   D   £31.00

3. The rectangle shown below has been divided into four rectangles with perimeters of 6 cm, 8 cm, 24 cm, and X cm. What is the value of X.

6	X
8	24

   A   16 cm   B   18 cm   C   20 cm   D   22 cm

4. You ran 2.15 km on Monday, 2.5 km on Wednesday, and 2.05 km on Friday. Which day did you run the farthest?

   _____

5. Karen went to the zoo and saw 25 monkeys, 12 eagles, 5 lions, and 16 turtles. What is the ratio of the eagles to the turtles?

   A   4:3   B   3:4   C   16:3   D   4:12

6. Luke held a birthday party. 8% of his visitors arrived late. If 18 visitors arrived late, how many attended Luke's birthday party?

   A   225   B   207   C   213   D   218

7. Jessy bought a box of pizza. She cut it into eight slices and gave her friend 1/4 of the pizza.

   How many slices of pizza were left for Jessy?

   A   5   B   6   C   3   D   7

8. Demi bought a dress and a bag and paid £224. The bag cost thrice as much as the dress. How much did they each cost?

   _____

   _____

9. Lily received thirteen 5p coins and sixteen 50p coins from her mom. Ali received three 5p coins and twenty-one 50p coins from his dad. Who received more money?

   _____

10. During summer, Michael reads 12 books. He reads p books in spring. During winter, he reads 5 more books than in spring. He read 33 books in total. How many books did he read during winter?

    A   15   B   16   C   8   D   13

TEST 35

1. Harry baked 8 chocolate chip cookies for his friends. The cookies weigh 237.325 grams in total.

   What is the mass of each chocolate chip cookie in kilograms? Round your answer to the nearest hundredths.

   _____

2. Albert receives his salary every 30 days. If he received his salary on a Friday, how many days will pass before Albert receives his salary again on a Friday?

   A   190 days   B   210 days   C   200 days   D   180 days

3. At a graduation ceremony, 6258 medals were given. Round off 6258 to the nearest tens.

   A   6260   B   6300   C   6250   D   6200

4. The HCF of m and 12 is 4. Their LCM is 24. What is the value of m?

   A   2   B   4   C   6   D   8

5. Sabrina is thinking of three consecutive numbers that have a sum equal to 57. What is the largest number?

   _____

6. Which of the following point is located on the X-axis?

    A $(0, 5)$ B $(3, 0)$ C $(2, -8)$ D $(-6, 7)$

7. If $4X + 3X = 21$ and $Y + Y + Y + Y = 36$. Find the value of $X \times Y$.

    A   27   B   21   C   26   D   36

8. Joe decides to save up money. He starts saving £4.50 on day 1. The money he saves increases by £2.40 every day. How much money will he save on the 15th day?

    A   £43.60   B   £38.10   C   £35.30   D   £25.50

9. A luggage case originally costs £60.00. How much would be the new price if the initial price is increased by $\frac{3}{16}$?

    A   £71.25   B   £85.00   C   £110.00   D   £82.60

10. A pot is $\frac{1}{8}$ full of water. When 2 liters of water is poured into it, it became $\frac{3}{4}$ full. How many liters of water can the pot contain?

_____

TEST 36

1. Julia found a rectangular cardboard with a perimeter of 40 in. If the width is 8 in, what is the area of the cardboard?

   _____

2. Patrick drew a figure that is made up of identical triangles as shown below.

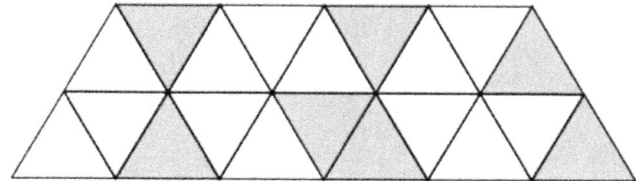

   What percentage of the figure is shaded?

   A   30%   B   35%   C   40%   D   55%

3. When Ashley cut a piece of cloth into equal pieces of $\frac{3}{4}$ cm, she had 8 pieces. How many $\frac{1}{3}$ cm pieces can she cut from the same cloth?

   A   14   B   16   C   20   D   18

4. Alex added a number to 5. Then he multiplied the sum by 4 and divided the product by 12. If the quotient is 15, what is the number?

   A   40   B   32   C   48   D   30

5. Olivia has 48 stamps which are 12 fewer than the number of stamps her brother Oliver has. What is the ratio of the number of stamps Oliver has to the total number of stamps both children have?

   A   4:3   B   4:5   C   4:7   D   5:9

6. On Saturday, Amelia knitted a sweater for $\frac{2}{3}$ hours. She took another $\frac{4}{5}$ hours on Sunday to completely knit the same sweater. How much time did she take knitting the sweater? Leave your answer as a mixed number in simplest form.

_____

7. Jacob had £100. He spent some money on 7 identical jackets and had £13.90 left. How much did each jacket cost?

   A   £13.90   B   £12.30   C   £12.90   D   £13.30

8. Which of the following can be the coordinates of points A and B?

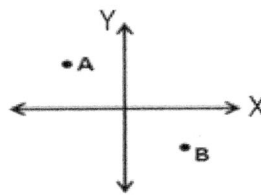

   A   A(4,-4)B(4,-4)   B   A(4,-4)B (-4,4)   C   A (-4,4) B (4,4)   D   A (-4, 4) B (4, -4)

9. A teacher asked Gavin and Rose to guess his height. Gavin estimated that his teacher's height is 186 cm and Rose's estimation was 190 cm. The teacher's height is 192.83 cm. Which of the two was more accurate?

_____

10. In a neighborhood, 5 houses own cats. House 1 takes care of seven cats, House 2 has three cats, House 3 has five cats, House 4 owns two cats and House 5 has eight cats. What is the average number of cats in the neighborhood?

   A   8   B   7   C   5   D   4

1. The table below shows the number of muffins that 42 customers ordered in May. The number of customers who ordered 5 muffins is not shown in the table.

Number of muffins	1	2	3	4	5
Number of customers	10	8	7	9	?

How many customers ordered at least 3 muffins in May?

A   10   B   28   C   19   D   24

2. 1000 sheets of paper have a thickness of 483 mm. How thick is each sheet of paper in centimeters?

A   0.483 cm   B   0.0483 cm   C   4.83 cm   D   0.00483 cm

3. Mary and Celeste baked 1000 brownies and decided to sell two brownies for £2.15. How much money will they have after selling all the brownies?

_____

4. Ron spent 1h 45min building shelves. He finished at 1:15 p.m. What time did he start building shelves?

A   11:30 a.m.   B   12:15 p.m.   C   10:30 a.m.   D   10:40 a.m.

5. A cinema has 18 rows with 10 seats in each row. If only $\frac{3}{5}$ of the seats were occupied, how many seats were empty?

A   85   B   94   C   108   D   72

6. Find all the prime factors of 1989.

_____

7. 35 liters of water is used to fill up bottles of 3 different capacities.

	Small	Medium	Large
	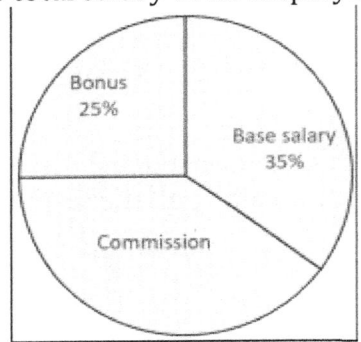		
Capacity	250 ml	500 ml	750 ml

There is an equal number of small-sized bottles and large-sized bottles. The number of medium-sized bottles is three times the number of small-sized bottles. How much water is used to fill up all the medium-sized bottles?

A   26 L   B   24 L   C   21 L   D   23

8. The pie chart below shows the total salary of an employee in a certain month.

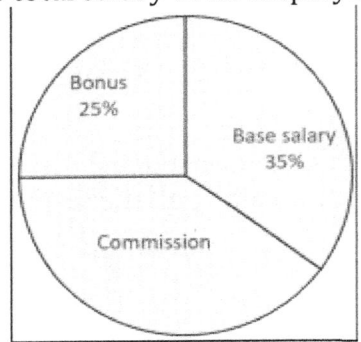

What would be the commission of the employee if the total amount earned by him in that month was £1000?

_____

9. Ben bought some apples to make three apple pies. Each pie needs 800 grams of apples. If each bag of apples weighs 0.40 kg, how many bags of apples did he buy?

A   5   B   6   C   7   D   8

10. Justin owns a round mirror. The diameter of the mirror is 14 centimeters. Find the area of the mirror.

A 49π cm^2 B 7π cm^2 C 14π cm^2 D π cm^2

TEST 38

1. What is the average mass of each cube, given that each cylinder weighs 0.35 kg?

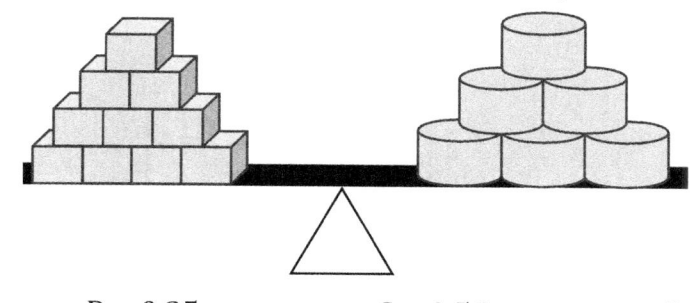

   A   0.21 kg   B   0.35   C   0.56 g   D   0.83 kg

2. Hailey's ballet lesson takes 2 hours 30 minutes every day. If the ballet lesson always starts at 15:15, what time does it end?

   A   19:15   B   5:45 p.m.   C   7:45 p.m.   D   17:15

3. A rectangular lawn is 24 m long and 15 m wide. If 6 m of its length is used as a pathway, how many meters must the width be increased to keep the same area?

   _____

4. The Venn diagram below shows the devices used by students in a classroom.

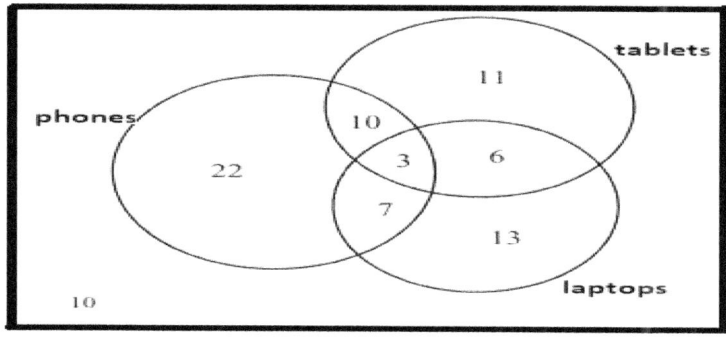

How many students use at least 2 devices?

   A   7   B   10   C   9   D   26

5. Matty has 80 toy cars. He buys more and has 100 toy cars now. What is the percentage increase in Matty's number of toy cars?

    A   25%   B   40%   C   75%   D   30%

6. Cassy measured her pencil and eraser.

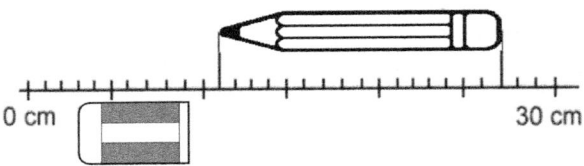

    How much longer is the pencil than the eraser?

    _____

7. Which of the following numbers is the least one?

    A   0   B   -46   C   -3   D   -17

8. Three kilograms of pears cost £33.00 while five kilograms of avocadoes cost £60.00. How much will you pay if you buy 6 kg of pears and 2 kg of avocadoes?

    A   £86.00   B   £92.00   C   £318.00   D   £90.00

9. Laura is making a bracelet. How many pearls will she need for 2 bracelets if she needs 12 pearls for $\frac{1}{4}$ of the bracelet?

    A   96   B   106   C   78   D   88

10. Teacher Alice wants to give 4 candies to each of her 32 students. How many packs of candies should she buy if a pack has 16 candies?

    A   9   B   10   C   8   D   12

1. MJ and NK are straight lines.
    ∠LON is a right angle. Find ∠LOM.

    A   45°   C   62°

    B   40°   D   58°

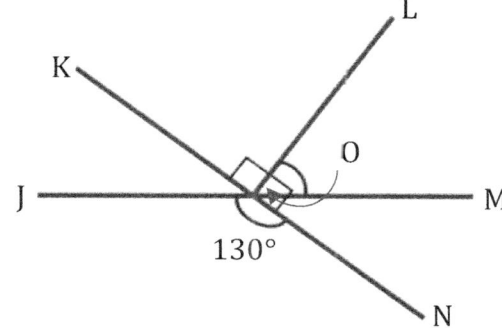

2. What is the mode of the following set of numbers: 13, 19, 2, 5, 7, 13, 13, 18, 19, 19, 21?

    A   13   B   19   C   21   D   Both A and B

3. Three boys went on biking on Saturday. Darren biked $8\frac{8}{15}$ km while Steve biked $\frac{207}{30}$ km, and Anthony biked $\frac{139}{18}$ km. Who cycled the farthest?

    A   Darren   B   Steve   C   Anthony   D   Both A and C

4. In a classroom, 14 students wear eyeglasses. If there are 35 students in the class, what percent of the class wears eyeglasses?

    _____

5. The protein-carbohydrate ratio in Miguel's diet in a day is 4:3. If he eats 250 grams of protein, how many grams of carbohydrates will he need to eat to balance his diet?

    A   175 grams   B   208.25 grams   C   193 grams   D   187.50 grams

6. Peter is three times older than his brother, who is 7 years old. Their mother's age is twice the sum of their ages. How old is their mother?

    A   46 years old   B   55 years old   C   56 years old   D   66 years old

7. A clock strikes at 3:30. Determine the type of angle formed between the clock's hands.

   A   Obtuse angle   B   Acute angle   C   Right angle   D   Straight angle

8. If you have 20-pence coins worth £65.80, how many coins do you have?

                                                                       _____

9. A box of 4 tarts comes with 1 free tart.

Buy 4, Get 1 **FREE!**

   If Hermione wants to buy 45 tarts, how many boxes of tarts should she buy?

                                                                       _____

10. In a meeting, 6 trays of soda can were consumed. Each tray has 15 cans, and each can of soda is 250 mL. How much soda (in liters) was consumed?

   A   2.25 L   B   22.5 L   C   245 L   D   24.5 L

1. A circle has a diameter of 17.2648 cm. What does 4 represent in 17.2648?

   A   4 tenths   B   4 hundreds   C   4 thousandths   D   4 hundredths

2. A pictogram shows the number of cupcakes sold in a bakeshop in three days.

Wednesday	🧁 🧁 🧁 🧁 🧁 🧁 🧁
Thursday	🧁 🧁 🧁 🧁
Friday	🧁 🧁 🧁 🧁 🧁 🧁 🧁
	🧁 = 6 cupcakes 🧁 = 3 cupcakes

How many cupcakes were sold in three days?

_____

3. If a cupcake costs £0.85, how much did the bakeshop earn on Wednesday?

   A   £20.85   B   £15.50   C   £17.85   D   £33.15

4. Team A's scores during their 10 basketball games were 85, 77, 93, 85, 90, 70, 73, 82, 78, and 69. Determine the median score of the team.

   A   80   B   82   C   78   D   85

5. What is the score of Team A on their 11th game if their average score is 82?

    _____

6. Find the values of x and y.

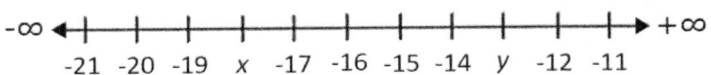

    A -25 and -22   B -18 and 13   C -18 and -13   D 18 and 13

7. Mandy has m pens. The number was doubled after her sister gave her unused pens. Her teacher gave her six more pens before she lost eleven pens. She divided the remaining pens into three to donate. Write an algebraic expression for the statement above.

    _____

8. Which of the following numbers is the greatest?

    A -235   B -627   C -31   D -89

9. Teacher Annie has 3 boxes of paper with x sheets of paper in each box. After giving each of her 15 students $\frac{1}{20}$ of the total sheets of paper, she was left with 60 sheets. How many sheets of paper did each student receive?

    A 20 sheets   B 12 sheets   C 18 sheets   D 10 sheets

10. Given $Z = 15x - 4x + 7k$, find the value of k if $Z = -36$ and $x = 5$.

    _____

TEST 41

1. A standard six sided dice is rolled twice. What is the probability that the sum of the two numbers on the dice is greater than 10?

   A $\frac{5}{6}$ B $\frac{1}{6}$ C $\frac{1}{36}$ D $\frac{1}{12}$

2. John played music on his phone for 36 minutes. What part of an hour did he play the music for?

   _____

3. A fruit vendor has six boxes that contain the same number of apples. How many apples are there in each box if there are a total of 192 apples?

   A 16 apples   B 32 apples   C 18 apples   D 14 apples

4. All prices are increased by 25%. What is the present price of an item that used to cost £140?

   _____

5. Jino can make 18 rag dolls in 8 days. At this rate, how long will it take him to make 135 dolls?

   A 60 days   B 45 days   C 30 days   D 55 days

6. Jacob drinks 250mL of fruit juice every day. How many days will it take him to finish a liter of fruit juice?

  A   5 days   B   8 days   C   4 Days   D   6 days

7. At £35 per square meter, what will be the cost of a rectangular lot 24m long and 15m wide?

```
        ┌─────────────────────────────────┐
        │                          15m     │
        │          24m                     │
        └─────────────────────────────────┘
```

  A   £12600   B   £1365   C   £2730   D   £25000

8. An octagon with equal sides has the same perimeter as that of a square. One side of the octagon is 36m. How long is one side of a square?

  _____

9. Jeremie scored 89 on the English test, 97 on the Math test, 95 on the Science test, 86 on the History test, and 95 on the Computer Test. What was her average score in all exams?

  A   94.2   B   98.6   C   98.4   D   92.4

10. A block of ice measures 80cm by 40cm by 25 cm. What is its volume?

  _____

TEST 42

1. What is the smallest number that gives 3 as a remainder when it is divided by 4, 6, and 7?

   A 87   B 84   C 86   D 85

2. A pit was dug in the form of a rectangular prism, having length of 8m, width of 6m, and depth of 3m. How much soil was taken from the pit?

   _____

3. Rexell recorded the distances she travelled with different modes of transportation as shown below. How much distance did she travel altogether in kilometers?

Mode of transportation	Distance
Walking	800m
Bus	5.2km
Train	60km
Airplane	524.5km
Car	8200m

   A 697.9 km   B 597.7 km   C 579.9 km   D 679.9 km

4. In 45, 923, 695 what is the place value of the underlined digit?

   _____

5. Dominique harvested $45\frac{3}{4}$ kg of potatoes and $36\frac{2}{3}$ kg of cabbages. How many more kilograms of potatoes did she harvest than cabbages?

_____

6. A fruit vendor has 195 grapes, 260 mangoes, 130 avocados and 65 melons to sell. What percent of the fruits are mangoes?

_____

7. During a mall sale, a pair of shoes marked £480 was bought for £320. What was the discount percentage?

   A   40%   B   66.67%   C   33.33%   D   32.46%

8. A point has coordinates (-3, 4). If it is translated 4 units to the right and 8 units downward, what are the new coordinates of that point?

_____

9. Trees are 250m apart. There are 6 trees along the road. What is the distance between the first and the last tree?

   A   1250 meters   B   1500 meters   C   1750 meters   D   1350 meters

10. If a car moves $15\frac{1}{2}$ km in 12minutes, what is the speed of the car in km per hour?

   A   67.5 kph   B   77.5 kph   C   75.5 kph   D   65.7 kph

TEST 43

1. One base angle of an isosceles triangle is 63°. Find the measure of the vertex angle.

   _____

2. Harry's residential lot is 420 square meters, while the adjacent lot owned by John is 800 square meters. Express the ratio of the lot owned by Harry to that of John in decimal form.

   _____

3. Jose created a pie chart to summarize the data he collected from the survey on what color do people like.

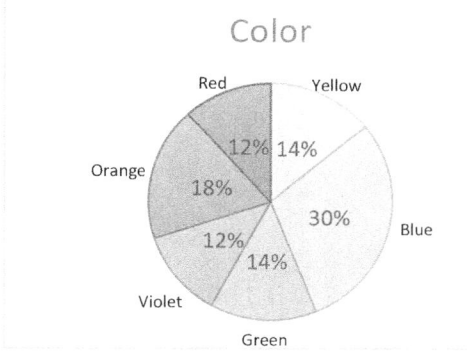

   If there are 25,000 respondents, how many people liked the color green?

   _____

4. An engineer wants to fence his pentagonal farm. If the sides of the farms are 24.5m, 65.23m, 12.05m, 65.3m and 9.57m. What is the total length that needs to be fenced?

   A   177.65 meters   B   174.45 meters   C   177.45 meters   D   176.65 meters

5. An egg costs £0.50. If Anne bought 12 dozen eggs and sold them at £0.75 each. How much was her profit from the sale?

   A   £48   B   £60   C   £45   D   £36

6. A piece of lumber is cut into two pieces. One piece is 1m longer than thrice the length of the other. If the total length of the lumber is 13m, what is the length of the longer piece?

   A   10 meters   B   12 meters   C   3 meters   D   13 meters

7. A set of a meal consists of a burger, fries, and a drink. A burger cost £12, a fries' cost £8 and a drink cost £3.50. If Ivet bought three sets of meals, how much was her change from £100?

   A   £32.50   B   £29.50   C   £38.50   D   £39.50

8. A famous Tiktoker has 2,284,573 followers. Round-off 2,284,573 to the nearest hundred thousand.

   _____

9. A game called Genshin Impact has a system called 'wish'. How many wishes can a player make in 13,600 primogems if each wish needs 160 primogems?

   A   95 wishes   B   75 wishes   C   85 wishes   D   86 wishes

10. Each tape record has 9345 seconds of recording. Express 9345 seconds in the form of hours, minutes, and seconds.

   _____

TEST 44

1. A swimming pool has dimensions 5m by 12m by 3m. Find the volume of the pool.

   _____

2. Maria has £6400 in her bank account in January. In February, she deposits £1250.50. Then in March, she deposits £500 but withdraws £352.65 after a week. If she wants to use all of her money for her birthday in April, how much money can she use for her birthday?

   A £7779.85　　　B £7977.85　　　C £7797.85　　　D £6797.85

3. The table below shows the predictions by different television stations on tomorrow's temperature.

Station	BBC	Nickelodeon	UKTV	ITV	CBS-AMC
Temperature	27.5 ºC	26.5 ºC	27 ºC	27.35 ºC	27.15 ºC

   What is the mean of the temperature predicted by five television stations?

   A 27.1 ºC　　　B 27 ºC　　　C 27.35 ºC　　　D 27.15 ºC

4. Write "seven hundred sixty-nine thousand four hundred fifty-five and fifteen hundredths"

   _____

5. A battery of a cellular phone has an energy span of 10 hours. Harry used 1hr 15min in the morning, 2hrs 45min in the afternoon and 3hrs 15min in the evening. If the battery was fully charged in the morning, what percent of charge in the battery was left?

   A 37.5%　　　B 26.5%　　　C 27.5%　　　D 25.7%

6. A rectangular tank contains 45 cubic meters of water. If the length and width of the tank are 4m and 5m respectively, how deep is the water in the tank?

_____

7. The Venn diagram below shows the number of students who played games.

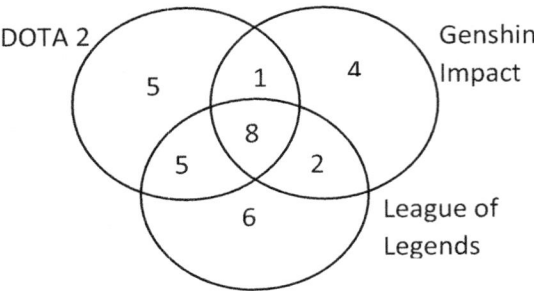

How many students played only 2 games?

_____

8. Charlotte has three franchising business. If she invested £120,000 in her first franchise and £563,250 in her second franchise. How much did she invest in her third franchise if her total investment was £800,000?

A £116750   B £125750   C £121750   D £118770

9. In creating a box, it requires 2 square meters of plywood and 0.25kg of nails. How much is the cost of two boxes if the plywood costs £20 per square meter and nails cost £30 per kg?

A £85   B £75   C £90   D £95

10. Five more than thrice a number is twice the difference between the number and two. What is twice that number?

_____

TEST 45

1. The time it takes Harvey to finish reading a book is 5days, 2hours and 36minutes. Immanuel can finish the same book in 4days, 18hours and 2minutes. What is the time difference between the two in minutes?

   A   618 minutes   B   725 minutes   C   475 minutes   D   514 minutes

2. It takes 15 minutes to completely fill the tank. How much water does the tank contain if the rate of water to fill the tank is 2.15 L/s?

   A   2725 liters   B   1935 liters   C   1275 liters   D   2235 liters

3. Armel drives $45\frac{3}{4}$ kilometers a day. He drove for $4\frac{2}{3}$ days. Determine the total distance he covered.

   A   213.5 km   B   217.5 km   C   188.5 km   D   220.5 km

4. What is the smallest number divisible by 12,13, and 15?

   _____

5. Each jump of a cat covers $1\frac{1}{2}$ meters. If the total distance covered by the cat by just jumping was 150meters, how many times did the cat jump?

   _____

6. A very popular meme was graded by different people from 1 (lowest) to 5 (highest). Ten responses were collected which were {3,4,5,3,5,2,5,2,3,5}. What was the mode of the data?

   A   3   B   4   C   5   D   2

7. A nonagon has nine equal sides. What is the perimeter of a nonagon if each side is 2.69meters?

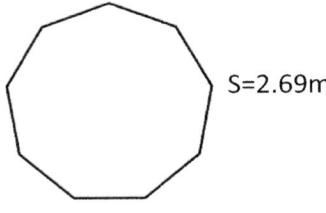

   S=2.69m

   _____

8. Jerry can eat $\frac{12}{17}$ of a whole cake. Saira can eat $\frac{23}{34}$ of the same cake. Who can eat the most cake?

   _____

9. An accountant has 155 pieces of $100-bill, 564 pieces of $10-bill, and 4867 pieces of $1-bill. How much money does the accountant have?

   A $25007   B $25006   C $25008   D $26007

10. The 5-meter pole casts a shadow of 2.5 meters. The building near the pole casts a shadow of 5.6 meters. How high is the building?

   _____

TEST 46

1. Mary has an average score of 88 in four tests. What is the needed score on the fifth test to get an average of 90?

   A 100   B 98   C 95   D 96

2. Arvie counted the number of mosquitos in a cage. The table below shows the number of mosquitos corresponding to the day they were counted.

Day	Number of mosquitos
1	12
2	24
3	48
4	96
5	192

   If the number of mosquitos has the same growth pattern each day, predict the number of mosquitos on the 8th day.

   _____

3. A notebook 1.2cm thick consists of 212 leaves of paper. Emman bought a 6cm thick notebook, how many leaves of paper are there?

   _____

4. A piece of plastic bag weighs 0.24g. Each pack of plastic bag consists of 50 plastic bags. What is the weight of seven packs of plastic bags?

   A 74 grams   B 88 grams   C 84 grams   D 92 grams

5. A window is formed from six pieces of rectangular plywood whose dimensions are 50cm by 20cm. What is the area of the formed window?

_____

6. Today, the value of a certain crypto coin is 3,546,789 pence. What digit is on the hundred-thousand place?

_____

7. Four dogs can eat 4 meals in 4 minutes. How many meals can a dog eat in an hour?

A   15 meals   B   60 meals   C   30 meals   D   45 meals

8. On Planet Earth, the gravity constant is 9.80665. Round-off to the nearest hundredths.

_____

9. Manny bought 25 meters of yarn. If each necklace needs 1.25 meters of yarn, how many necklaces can she make?

A   20 necklaces   B   24 necklaces   C   25 necklaces   D   28 necklaces

10. A treasure hunter went to the X-mark and found a treasure map. If each centimeter in the map is 2,500m in reality, what is the distance in the map between the X-mark and the treasure if the total distance, in reality was 24,525 meters?

A   12.21 cm   B   8.91 cm   C   9.84 cm   D   9.81 cm

TEST 47

1. Joseph can shoot 15 arrows in a minute, while Jacob can shoot 13 arrows in a minute. They both start shooting arrows together. How many arrows were shot in total after 28 minutes?

   _____

2. A cube has six equal square faces. If the side of a cube is 12 meters, what is the total surface area of the cube?

   A   712 m²   B   854 m²   C   864 m²   D   866 m²

3. Each egg case of an insect consists of 50 eggs. If the insect can lay three egg cases every week, how many eggs can be produced by the insect in four weeks?

   _____

4. A bell rings every 45 minutes. Another bell rings every hour. If the two bells ring together at 11:00 AM, at what time will they ring together again?

   A   2:00 PM   B   3:00 PM   C   3:30 PM   D   2:15 PM

5. A tank is filled with oil. After 76L of oil was drawn out, the tank is $\frac{3}{5}$ full. How many liters of oil can the tank hold?

   _____

6. Jake wrote the whole numbers 16, 8, 6, 28, 26, and 18 on the faces of a cube. Every pair of opposite faces has the same sum. What is the sum?

   _____

7. From a rectangular cardboard, a small rectangle is cut out as shown in the figure below. Find the perimeter of the remaining cardboard.

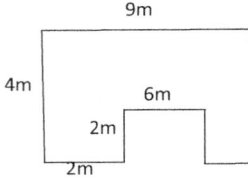

   A   15 meters   B   23 meters   C   26 meters   D   30 meters

8.   Shakira measured the length of a pole to be 5.65 meters. If the true length of the pole is 5.6835 meters, what is the error in the measured length?

   _____

9. Monica has £250 in her wallet. She bought two flowers which cost £35.50 each and three pots which cost £25.50 each. How much money was left?

   A   £102.50   B   £120.50   C   £112.50   D   £121.50

10. A photocopier can produce 150 copies in a minute. How many minutes will it take to produce 5250 copies?

   A   45 minutes   B   35 minutes   C   25 minutes   D   30 minutes

1. A cake factory can produce 155 cakes in a single day. If each cake sells for £63.54, how much money can be made in a week if all cakes are sold?

   A £59092.20   B £9848.70   C £68940.90   D £444.78

2. A thesis study was conducted by three students. Anniel finished $\frac{1}{12}$ part more than Jacob and $\frac{1}{18}$ part less than Jeremie. What part of the study did Anniel finish?

   A $\frac{37}{108}$ B $\frac{43}{108}$ C $\frac{7}{27}$ D $\frac{5}{36}$

3. A TV series contains 12 episodes. Yves can watch 10 episodes in a single day. How many days will it take him to watch 5 series, if all of them contain the same number of episodes of equal length?

   _____

4. A firetruck hose can release 25 liters per minute to prevent fire from spreading. On a certain day, a wildfire spread in the forest. Firefighters used the fire truck to stop the fire from spreading. It took 1 hour and 25 minutes to stop the fire. How much water was used?

   A 2250 liters   B 2425 liters   C 2225 liters   D 2125 liters

5. An electric fan can rotate at an average speed of 500 turns per second. How many turns can it make in 1 hour?

   _____

6. There are balls with different colors inside an urn (2red, 3blue, 4white, 5green, and 6black). One ball was drawn randomly. What is the probability that the ball was blue? Give your answer as a percentage.

_____

7. Two unbiased dice numbered from one to six were tossed. What is the probability that the sum of the numbers on the two dice is seven?

_____

8. What is the perimeter of an equilateral triangle if each side has a length of 56 units?

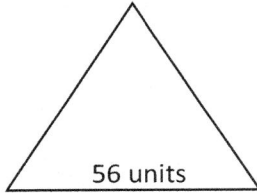

56 units

_____

9. A certain brownie recipe needs $\frac{3}{8}$ cup of sugar and is good for 4 persons. How many cups of sugar are needed to make brownies for 16 persons?

   A $1\frac{1}{2}$ cup   B $1\frac{3}{8}$ cup   C $1\frac{1}{4}$ cup   D $1\frac{1}{6}$ cup

10. An electric fan has an energy consumption of 35 kilowatts per hour, a light bulb has an energy consumption of 12 kilowatts per hour, and a charger has an energy consumption of 8 kilowatts per hour. How many kilowatts were consumed if all appliances were operated for 4.5 hours?

   A   247.5 kW   B   217.5 kW   C   227.5 kW   D   237.5 kW

TEST 49

1. Jose picked 25% more oranges than Emman did. If Emman picked 120 oranges, how many oranges did Jose pick?

   _____

2. A cloth has dimensions 4m by 5m. How many 0.5m by 0.5m pieces can be cut from the cloth?

   _____

3. Johnson borrowed £18500 from the bank at a 9% simple interest rate per annum. He needs to pay back the borrowed amount plus interest at the end of the year. If he pays £9000 at the end of the year, how much more does he need to pay?

   A   £11,165   B   £6800   C   £16800   D   £12265

4. The figures are made up of equal squares. If Figure A has a perimeter of 108cm, what is the perimeter of the Figure B?

   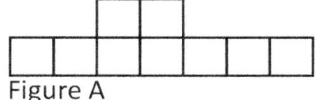

   A   54 cm   B   84 cm   C   64 cm   D   74 cm

5. A block of ice can freeze completely in 5 hours. What percentage of the ice block is frozen after 3.75 hours?

   A   85%   B   75%   C   65%   D   66.67%

6. There are 76,294 bacteria in a contaminated drink. Express 76,294 in expanded form.

    _____

7. A man wishes to save money for buying a house. If he saves £5000 per year, how much money will he have after 18 years?

    _____

8. The accuracy of an arrow to hit its target is 20%. If an archer draws 125 arrows, how many targets will be hit?

    A   105 targets   B   60 targets   C   50 targets   D   25 targets

9. A certain class has tallied the grade vs. the number who got that grade in a table shown.

Grade	A	B	C	D	E
No. of Students	12	35	76	25	18

    If A is the highest grade and E is the lowest grade, how many students have a grade below B?

    _____

10. What is the area of the figure left unshaded if the big and small squares have side 5cm and 3.5cm, respectively?

    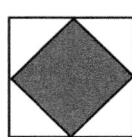

    A   2.25 m²   B   12.25 m²   C   72.25 m²   D   12.75 m²

TEST 50

1. Mary summarized her expenses in buying things in the table shown below.

Things	Cost each item	Number of items
Shampoo	£5.0	1
Cologne	£14.5	2
Soap	£3.6	5
Toothpaste	£2.5	2
Toothbrush	£3.0	1

If she paid £100, how much change did she get?

A   £60   B   £40   C   £30   D   £50

2. Stephen Curry has a shooting rate of 90% in a free throw in basketball. How many successful shots did he make in 650 free throws?

A   585 shots   B   65 shots   C   650 shots   D   600 shots

3. An airplane takes 3 hours 52 minutes 36 seconds to arrive at Singapore from Manila. From Singapore Airport to Hotel, it takes 2 hours 12 minutes and 43 seconds. What is the total time travelled?

_____

4. Sara and Maria ran in the opposite direction at a speed of 25kph and 27.5 kph, respectively. If they started at the same place, what is the distance between them after 1 hour and 30 minutes?

A   76.5 km   B   75.50 km   C   78.75 km   D   77.85 km

5. An urn contains 4 white balls, 5 black balls and 12 red balls. If one ball is picked at random, what is the probability of getting a white or a black ball?

_____

6. One angle of a triangle measures 15° more than twice the second angle. The third angle measures 10° more than the first angle. What is the angle measure of the second angle?

A 71°   B 81°   C 38°   D 28°

7. A rectangle has a length that measures 2m less than thrice its width. If the perimeter of the rectangle is 44m, what is the area of the rectangle?

_____

8. The formula of the area of a circle is $A = \pi r^2$. If the circle has a radius of 7m, what is the area of the circle?
(Note: $\pi = 22/7$)

_____

9. Rem was saving coins for her to buy her favorite food. She saved £1 on the first day, £2 on the second day, £3 on the third day and so on. How much money did she have saved after one week?

A £28   B £6   C £42   D £35

10. Ram cut the $5\frac{7}{12}$ ft lumber into two parts. One part is $1\frac{6}{7}$ ft long. What is the length of the other part?

_____

1. An ant colony triples every week. If there are 1250 ants in a colony, then how many ants will be there after four weeks?

    A   3750 ants   B   15000 ants   C   101250 ants   D   45000 ants

2. A table has a height of 1.2meters, a book has a thickness of 4cm, and a cat has a height of 20cm when sitting. What is the total height when a cat is sitting on two books placed on top of the table?

    _____

3. An apple contains 95% water. If an apple has a volume of 300 cm^3, how much water is contained in 20 apples?

    _____

4. During a particular Festival, 11546 people attended every day and each ate two servings of fried chicken. If the festival lasted for two weeks, how many servings of fried chicken were eaten?

    A   323288   B   23092   C   161644   D   484932

5. If the weight of a person, W, in Newton has a function W=9.81×m, where m is the mass of a person. What would be the weight of a person having a mass of 40 kg?

    _____

6. A farmer gathered 4256 flowers. If he sold them at £25 for every 8 pieces of flower, how much did he earn from selling all the flowers?

    A   £851200   B   £13600   C   £13300   D   £106400

7. Amiel gets a commission of £250 from his sales. If this is 5% of his sales, how much are his total sales?

    A   £263.16   B   £262.50   C   £8000   D   £5000

8. If $\frac{41}{5}$ is added to a certain number, the result will be $8\frac{8}{15}$. What is that number?

    _____

9. A rectangular tray has a length of 10 dm, a width of 9 dm and a height of 12 dm. How much water can it hold? [Figure not drawn to scale]

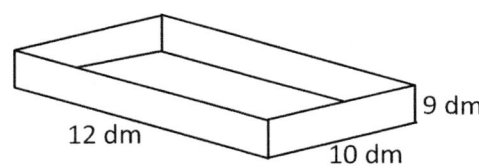

    A   360 dm³   B   31 dm³   C   108 dm³   D   1024 dm³

10. Harvey is having a problem with getting the prime factorization of 360. What is the prime factorization of 360?

    _____

TEST 52

1. Jino conducted a survey at an Elementary school. The table shown below represents the number of boys and girls for each grade.

	Boys	Girls
Grade 1	34	72
Grade 2	65	61
Grade 3	43	55
Grade 4	54	63
Grade 5	26	75

How many students are there in total?

_____

2. A square meter of a wall consists of 12.5 hollow blocks. How many hollow blocks are needed if a house has a total wall area of 72.4 square meters?

A   905   B   1250   C   860   D   1150

3. A watch is worth £1560. If it was sold with a discount of 20%, how much was it sold for?

_____

4. An aquarium is 1.5 m long, 0.55 m wide and 0.45 m deep. How many liters of water does it contain when it is $\frac{2}{3}$ full?

A   0.2275 m³   B   0.2475 m³   C   0.1250 m³   D   0.250 m³

5. What is the next term in the sequence: 1, 8 ,27, 64, __?

_____

6. What is 10% of 25% of the product of 8 and 15?

_____

7. Today, my brother is twice as old as I am. How old is my brother after 10 years if today I am 5 years old?

   A   15 years old   B   30 years old   C   20 years old   D   25 years old

8. A point has coordinates of (-2, 4). It moves 2 units to the left and 1 unit downwards. Then it again moves 3 units to the right and 3 units downwards. What are the new coordinates of that point?

_____

9. A can of paint can color 20 square meters with a single coating. How many cans of paint are needed to color a wall with 1260 square meters with 4 coatings?

   A   126 cans   B   504 cans   C   252 cans   D   475 cans

10. A Frog eats 50 insects a day. In a certain area, there are 25 frogs and 26250 insects. For how many days will the insects last before they are all eaten by the frogs?

   A   14 days   B   21 days   C   7 days   D   18 days

1. A cup of coffee contains 5% sugar. How much sugar is needed for 12 cups if each cup contains 300g of coffee?

   A   18g   B   15g   C   180g   D   150g

2. Saira runs at a speed of 9 kilometer per hour. How long will it take for her to run 1.2 kilometers in minutes?

   _____

3. Jackets have a variety of sizes. Each size is 8cm longer than the adjacent smaller size. If the categories of sizes are XL, L, M, S, and XS, what is the size of XS if the size of XL is 1.2 meters?

   A   30.8m   B   0.88m   C   1.52m   D   0.86m

4. Jeremie is making a sweet drink. She uses 50g of sugar, 125.75g of mango powder, 80g of milk and 1.2kg of water to make the drink. What is the total weight of the drink in grams?

   _____

5. A battalion consists of a platoon leader and 200 soldiers. An army consisting of 156400 soldiers is prepared for war. How many platoon leaders are needed for the war?

   _____

6. During rainfall, a tank collects 200 cm³ per minute. If it rains for 3.15 hours, how much water is collected by the tank?

_____

7. For every 12 light bulbs produced by a factory, one bulb is defective. If a company orders 408 light bulbs, how many bulbs will <u>not</u> be defective?

    A   384 bulbs   B   374 bulbs   C   396 bulbs   D   348 bulbs

8. A hospital conducted a survey in which the patients, male and female, describe the experience of their hospital stay.

	Good	Bad
Male	45	12
Female	20	54

If a patient is selected at random, what is the probability of selecting a male who had a 'Bad' experience?

    A $\frac{12}{131}$ B $\frac{54}{131}$ C $\frac{20}{131}$ D $\frac{45}{131}$

9. An angle measures 135°. It is divided into two parts in which one part is four times the other. What is the measure of the largest angle?

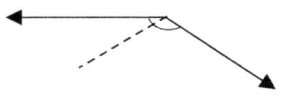

_____

10. Last Saturday, Jacob went to a cinema. He had £120. He paid £7.5 for his movie ticket and £2.8 for his popcorn. How much money was left?

    A   £107.9   B   £109.7   C   £112.5   D   £115

TEST 54

1. Dominique is taking a 255 km bicycle trip. Each day she rides her bike for 15 km. How many days does it take Dominique to finish the trip?

   _____

2. Emmanuel is making a pattern with squares as shown below.

   Row 1
   Row 2
   Row 3
   Row 4

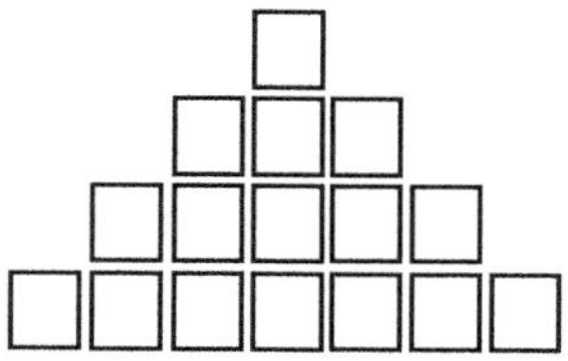

   If Emmanuel continues the pattern, how many squares will be at Row 6?

   A   9   B   13   C   10   D   11

3. Anniel participated in a track and field event at his school. In the long jump, he jumped 48 inches. How many feet did Anniel jump?
   (Note: 1 foot = 12 inches)

   A   4 ft   B   3 ft   C   2 ft   D   5 ft

4. A butterfly has a life span of 3 days. If a butterfly has lived 70 hours, how many more hours will the butterfly live?

   A   72 hours   B   12 hours   C   15 hours   D   2 hours

5. A man can carry 50kg of bricks. If a brick weighs 250g, how many bricks can a man carry?

   _____

6. The bar graph below shows the number of people who bought an iPhone X in 4 months.

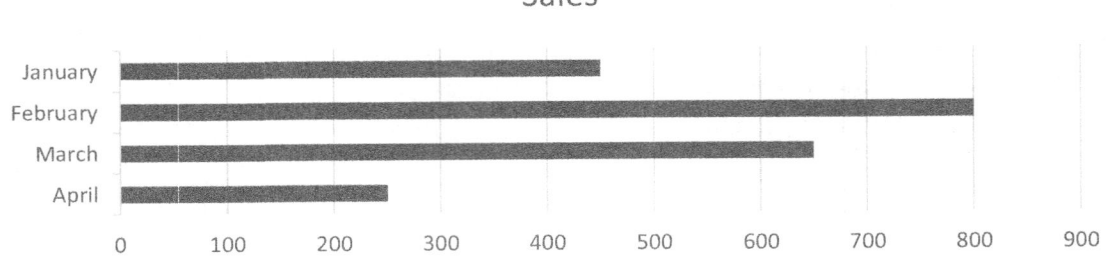

How many more iPhone X were bought in January than in April?

_____

7. Yves bought $5\frac{1}{2}$kg of meat while Jino bought $8\frac{2}{3}$kg of meat. How much more meat did Jino buy compared to Yves?

A $1\frac{1}{3}$kg   B $3\frac{1}{6}$ kg   C $2\frac{1}{6}$ kg   D $2\frac{1}{3}$kg

8. A big aquarium has 651, 623 fish. Round-off to the nearest ten thousands.

_____

9. A marble weighs 50g and a jar weighs 1.2 kg. If a jar containing marbles weighs 9.6kg, how many marbles are there inside the jar?

A   172 marbles   B   148 marbles   C   168 marbles   D   178 marbles

10. Rex read 8 books last month. Each book had 32 pages. How many pages did Rex read?

_____

TEST 55

1. A jar contains 50 candies with different flavors. If there are 12 chocolate candies, what is the probability of NOT picking chocolate candies?

    A $\frac{39}{50}$ B $\frac{6}{25}$ C $\frac{18}{25}$ D $\frac{19}{25}$

2. On 5 exams in mathematics, a student scored 82, 93, 86, 92, and 79. Find the median score.

    _____

3. A triangle has a base of 12meters and a height of 5 meters, what is the area of this triangle?

    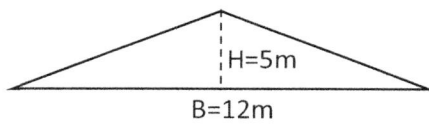

    _____

4. A rectangular container can carry 6 m³ of water. If the dimensions of the length and width are 4m by 3m, what must be the height of that container?

    A 0.4 m   B 0.5 m   C 0.6 m   D 0.8 m

5. Jake earned £2,651,659 for five years. What is the place value of the underlined number?

    _____

6. A dog eats thrice as much as a cat. Manny owns a cat and a dog. How much food does he need if a cat eats 500g of food?

    _____

7. During hot weather, John measured the temperature to be 43.64°C. If the reading of an accurate digital thermometer was 45.12°C, how much was John's error in measuring the temperature?

    A   0.48 °C   B   1.48 °C   C   0.38 °C   D   1.38 °C

8. Jo's father gave her an amount equivalent to $\frac{3}{4}$ of her saving in order to buy a phone. If her savings was £500, and she spent all her money to buy the phone, how much did the phone cost?

    A   £375   B   £625   C   £875   D   £775

9. In a group of 90 teenagers, one-third are girls and the remaining are boys. Three-fourths of the boys wear long pants. Two-thirds of the boys wearing long pants wear shoes. How many boys wear long pants with shoes?

    A   30   B   15   C   10   D   45

10. Two numbers when added are equal to 135. What is the difference between them if one number is 59?

    _____

ANSWERS
and
SOLUTIONS

TEST 1 SOLUTION

1. A. 2.4 hrs
   Solution:
   In 1 hour:
   Pipe A will fill 1/4 of the tank and
   Pipe B will fill 1/6 of the tank.
   Together, they will fill $1/4 + 1/6$
   $= 5/12$ of the tank in 1 hour.
   Hence they will take $12/5 = 2.4$
   hours to fill the whole tank.

2. C. 42
   Solution:
   Sum of 80 numbers,
   $80 \times 55 = 4400$
   Sum of remaining 78 numbers,
   $4400 - 274 - 850 = 3276$
   Mean of 78 numbers,
   $3276 \div 78 = 42$

3. B. 2000m
   Solution:
   Speed of Mazda,
   $10000 \div 40 = 250$m/min
   Speed of Toyota,
   $10000 \div 50 = 200$m/min
   After Mazda reached the finish
   line, Toyota still travelled for 10
   minutes.
   Distance travelled = 200 x 10
   = 2000m

4. A. 7 yrs
   Solution:
   $41 + N = 3 \times (9 + N)$
   $41 + N = 27 + 3N$
   $N = 7$

5. B. £9.60
   Solution:
   $120\% \times N = 14.14$
   $N = 12$
   $12 - 20\% \times 12 = 9.60$

6. B. 4500 seconds
   Solution:
   Time difference,
   15hrs 00min – 13hrs 45min
   =1hr 15min
   $1hr \times 3600 + 15 \times 60 = 4500$sec

7. A. 190
   Solution:
   11am = 75
   12pm = 50
   1pm = 65
   $75 + 50 + 65 = 190$

8. B. £1500
   Solution:
   $18 \times £50 + 15 \times £20 + 30 \times £10$
   $= £1500$

9. D. 2048
   Solution:
   $1^{st} = 4 = 2 \times 2 = 2^{1+1}$
   $2^{nd} = 8 = 2 \times 2 \times 2 = 2^{2+1}$
   $3^{rd} = 16 = 2 \times 2 \times 2 \times 2 = 2^{3+1}$
   $4^{th} = 32 = 2 \times 2 \times 2 \times 2 \times 2 = 2^{4+1}$
   . . .
   $10^{th} = 2^{10+1} = 2048$

10. 184 m^2
    Solution:
    Area of rectangle = 12x16 = 192
    Area of missing triangle:
    $= ½ \times 4 \times 4 = 8$
    Area of the shape:
    $= 192 - 8 = 184$ m^2

TEST 2 SOLUTION

1. D. All three

   Solution:

   For original data, the mode (most occurred value) is 14, median (middle value) is also 14, and mean (average) is also 14. With the addition of 14 to the data set, all three values remain the same.

2. C. 128 m²

   Solution:

   Area of field $= s^2 = 12 \times 12 = 144$

   Area of pit $= 4 \times 4 = 16$

   Remaining area $= 144 - 16 = 128$ m²

3. C. $\frac{1}{36}$

   Solution:

   Probability of getting six on first dice $= \frac{1}{6}$

   Probability of getting six on second dice $= \frac{1}{6}$

   Combined probability of two sixes $= \frac{1}{6} \times \frac{1}{6} = \frac{1}{36}$

4. A. Improper fraction

   Solution:

   $\frac{P}{q}$ is a proper fraction if $p < q$

   But 69=69. Therefore, improper.

5. C. $\frac{12}{11}$

   Solution:

   $$n \times \frac{2}{3} = \frac{8}{11}$$

   $$n = \frac{8}{11} \div \frac{2}{3}$$

   $$n = \frac{8}{11} \times \frac{3}{2} = \frac{24}{22}$$

   $$n = \frac{24 \div 2}{22 \div 2} = \frac{12}{11}$$

6. $\frac{5}{12}$

   Solution:

   The Lowest Common Denominator of 8 and 12 is 24

   $$\frac{3}{8} \times \frac{3}{3} = \frac{9}{24}$$

   $$\frac{5}{12} \times \frac{2}{2} = \frac{10}{24}$$

   $$\frac{9}{24} < \frac{10}{24}$$

7. D. $\frac{73}{15}$

   Solution:

   $$3\frac{4}{5} + N = 8\frac{2}{3}$$

   $$N = 8\frac{2}{3} - 3\frac{4}{5}$$

   $$N = \frac{26}{3} - \frac{19}{5}$$

   $$\frac{130}{15} - \frac{57}{15} = \frac{73}{15}$$

8. 75%

   Solution:

   $$\frac{3}{4} = 3 \div 4 = 0.75$$

   $$0.75 \div 100 = 75\%$$

9. C. 60 marbles

   Solution:

   $50\% \, y = 30$

   $y = 30 \div 50\%$

   $y = 30 \div 0.5$

   $y = 60$

10. B. 4:3

    Solution:

    $$\frac{32}{24} = \frac{32 \div 8}{24 \div 8} = \frac{4}{3}$$

    $$\frac{4}{3} = 4:3$$

TEST 3 SOLUTION

1. A. 150 days
   Solution:
   $$\frac{12}{40} = \frac{N}{500}$$
   $$N = \frac{(12 \times 500)}{40} = 150$$

2. B. 36m x 27m
   Solution:
   $24 \times 1.5 = 36$
   $18 \times 1.5 = 27$

3. C. 2J – 2

4. C. 42
   Solution:
   $N = (85 – 58) + 15$
   $N = 27 + 15$
   $N = 42$

5. C. 25 seats
   Solution:
   $13-10 = 3$
   $16-13 = 3$
   The pattern repeats
   4th row: 16+3=19
   5th row: 19+3=22
   6th row: 22+3 = 25

6. D. 16,584 seconds
   Solution:
   $4\text{hours} \times 60 \times 60 = 14400$
   $36\text{minutes} \times 60 = 2160$
   24seconds
   Total $= 16584$

7. C. (0, 9)
   Solution:
   The point (0, 9) has values x = 0, and y = 9, which means that it is located on y-axis.

8. B. 150 liters
   Solution:
   $750\text{mL} \div 1000 = 0.75\text{L}$
   $0.75 \times 200 = 150$

9. 1.53 meters
   Solution:
   $149 + 4 = 153\text{cm}$
   $153\text{cm} \div 100 = 1.53\text{m}$

10. B. 30 degrees
    Solution:
    Let N be the angle
    Complement angle $= 2N$
    $N + 2N = 90$
    $3N = 90$
    $N = 30$

TEST 4 SOLUTION

1. A. Thousands
   Solution:
   5,000 is 5×1,000
   1,000 is thousands

2. D. -8
   Solution:
   Arrange from least to greatest
   -87, -38, -34, -8, -3, 2, 6
   The middle number is -8

3. Hundred thousandths
   Solution:
   $4 \times \dfrac{1}{100,000} = 0.00004$
   $\dfrac{1}{100,000}$ is hundred thousandths

4. 300,000,000
   Solution:
   The hundred millions place is 2
   The number on the right of 2 is 9
   which is greater than or equal to
   5.
   2|99 792 458 = 2+1 | 00 000 000
   Therefore, 300,000,000

5. Jacob
   Solution:
   Jacob: 5.661 – 5.645 = 0.016
   Anniel: 5.661 – 5.695 = - 0.034
   0.016 is nearer closer to zero than
   -0.034. Therefore, Jacob is more
   accurate.

6. D. (1, 1)
   Solution:
   One point is on the origin, and the
   other two are only 1 unit away
   from the origin. The point (1, 1) is
   farthest from the origin as its
   distance is more than 1 unit
   i.e. $\sqrt{(1^2 + 1^2)} = 1.414$ units

7. A. 64 tiles
   Solution:
   tiles = s^2
   tiles = 8×8
   tiles = 64

8. $\dfrac{2}{3}$
   Solution:
   10 and 15 has a common factor of
   5
   $\dfrac{10}{15} = \dfrac{10 \div 5}{15 \div 5} = \dfrac{2}{3}$

9. B. ½
   Solution:
   Total cards in a deck=52
   Total red cards in a deck = 26
   Probability of getting a red card =
   26/52 = ½

10. C. $\dfrac{4}{15}$
    Solution:
    $\dfrac{8}{15} \times \dfrac{1}{2} = \dfrac{8}{30} = \dfrac{4}{15}$

TEST 5 SOLUTION

1. B. $\frac{17}{8}$ or $2\frac{1}{8}$ pounds

   Solution:

   The LCD of 4,2, and 8 is 8

   $\frac{3}{4} = \frac{6}{8}; \frac{1}{2} = \frac{4}{8}; \frac{7}{8}$

   $\frac{6}{8} + \frac{4}{8} + \frac{7}{8} = \frac{17}{8}$

   $\frac{17}{8} = 2\frac{1}{8}$

2. $\frac{29}{8}$ or $3\frac{5}{8}$

   Solution:

   $10 - 6\frac{3}{8} = 10 - \frac{8 \times 6 + 3}{8}$

   $\frac{80 - 51}{8} = \frac{29}{8}$ or $3\frac{5}{8}$

3. $\frac{2}{5}$

   Solution:

   $40\% \div 100\% = \frac{40}{100}$

   $\frac{40 \div 20}{100 \div 20} = \frac{2}{5}$

4. A. 28

   Solution:

   Number of correct answers,

   $80 \times 65\%$

   $80 \times 0.65 = 52$

   Number of incorrect answers,

   $80 - 52 = 28$

5. 1cm

   Solution:

   Volume = height X length X width

   $30cm^3 = 5cm \times 6cm \times (x)$

   $30cm^3 = 30cm^2 (x)$

   $x = 1cm$

6. C. 84 sandwiches

   Solution:

   $\frac{7 sandwiches}{1 loaf} = \frac{N}{12 loaf}$

   $N = 7 \times 12 = 84$

7. $\frac{35 + N}{N}$

8. $A = 110$ m²

   Solution:

   Area of whole figure = 15 x 10 = 150m²

   Area of triangle = 10 x 8 x ½ = 40m²

   Area of shaded region:

   = 150 – 40 = 110 m²

9. C. 70 seconds

   Solution:

   $\frac{100m}{20sec} = \frac{350}{N}$

   $N = 350 \times \frac{20}{100} = 70$

10. A. 86400 sec

    Solution:

    $1 day \times 24\frac{hr}{day} \times 60\frac{min}{hr} \times 60\frac{sec}{min}$

    $= 86400$

TEST 6 SOLUTION

1. C. -22

   Solution

   The possible number between -23 and -20 is -22 and -21 only.

2. B. 44,000

   Solution:

   Thousands place is 3

   The number on the right of 3 is 5 which is greater than or equal to 5

   43|564 = 43+1|000

   Therefore, 44,000

3. B. 0.05 degrees Celsius

   Solution:

   24.5 – 24.45 = 0.05

4. B. 18

   Solution:

   The product of two negative numbers is a positive number

   $(-4.5) \times (-4) = 18$

5. C. 9990

   LCM of 2,3,5,6 is 30

   The number we need must be divisible by 30.

   Amongst the answer choices, the largest such 4 digit number is 9990.

6. $\frac{8}{9}$

   Solution:

   The LCD of 9 and 7 is 63

   $\frac{8}{9} = \frac{56}{63}; \frac{6}{7} = \frac{54}{63}$

   $\frac{56}{63} > \frac{54}{63}$

7. $22^2 - 55^2$

8. 4.

   Solution:

   Arrange the data set in ascending order: 1, 1, 2, 3, 4, 4, 5, 6, 7, 9

   Since the data set has even numbers in total, hence there will be two middle numbers. However, as both middle numbers are 4, hence the median is 4.

9. B. 25%

   Solution:

   Probability of two Heads when coin is tossed two times = ½ x ½ = ¼ , which is also equal to 25%

10. C. £160

    Solution:

    Cost of blouse,

    B = 0.8S

    Total cost

    B + S = 360

    0.8S + S = 360

    1.8S = 360

    S = 360÷1.8 = 200

    B = 0.8S = 0.8×200 = 160

TEST 7 SOLUTION

1. A. $1\times10,000 + 2\times1,000 + 4\times10 + 5$
   Solution:
   $1\times10,000 + 2\times1,000 + 4\times10 + 5$
   $= 10,000 + 2,000 + 40 + 5$
   $= 12,045$

2. B. $\frac{10}{19}$
   Solution:
   No. of red marbles $= 10$
   Total no. of marbles $= 19$
   Probability of picking a red
   marble $= \frac{10}{19}$

3. C. £192
   Solution:
   Number of bags,
   $96 \div 12 = 8$
   Total cost,
   $8\times24 = 192$

4. D. 105
   Solution:
   Since 3, 5, and 7 are all prime
   numbers. Therefore LCM =
   $3\times5\times7 = 105$

5. $\frac{5}{12}, \frac{5}{11}, \frac{5}{10}, \frac{5}{9}$
   Solution:
   Since all numerators are the same.
   Then, the lowest fraction is the
   one with highest value at the
   denominator.

6. B. 12.5%
   Solution:
   $\frac{1}{8} = 1\div8 = 0.125$
   $0.125 \times 100\% = 12.5\%$

7. A. 8%
   Solution:
   Area of green portion $= \frac{1}{4} = 25\%$
   Area of White portion $= 33\%$
   Area of Red portion $= 17\%$
   Area of Grey portion $= 17\%$
   So, area of blue portion =
   $= 100 - 25 - 33 - 17 - 17 = 8\%$

8. $\frac{3}{4}N - 5 = 10$

9. A. 85m by 22m
   Solution:
   $L = 4W - 3$
   Perimeter,
   $2\times(L+W) = 214$
   $L + W = 214\div2$
   $4W - 3 + W = 107$
   $5W = 107+3$
   $5W = 110$
   $W = 110\div5$
   $W = 22$
   $L = 4\times22 - 3 = 85$

10. C. 1.345kg
    Solution:
    Convert grams to kg,
    $76,345g = 76.345kg$
    Difference in weight,

$$76.345 - 75 = 1.345$$

TEST 8 SOLUTION

1. D. Ten thousandths
   Solution:
   $$0.0004 = 4 \times \frac{1}{10,000}$$
   $\frac{1}{10,000}$ is ten thousandths

2. D. 13
   Solution:
   $$1155 = 3 \times 5 \times 7 \times 11$$
   13 is not a factor of 1155

3. A. 16
   Solution:
   Let N be the number.
   Mistake,
   $$N^3 = 64$$
   $$N = 4$$
   Correct,
   $$N^2 = 4^2 = 16$$

4. 6
   Solution:
   'Mode' is the number that occurs most frequently. Since it is given that the number '6' occurred more than any other number, hence '6' is the mode of this data set.

5. D. 64 dresses
   Solution:
   $$40 \div \frac{5}{8} = 40 \times \frac{8}{5}$$
   $$\frac{320}{5} = 64$$

6. $\frac{111}{35}$ or $3\frac{6}{35}$
   Solution:
   $$3\frac{4}{7} - \frac{2}{5} = \frac{7 \times 3 + 4}{7} - \frac{2}{5}$$
   $$\frac{25}{7} - \frac{2}{5} = \frac{25 \times 5 - 2 \times 7}{35}$$
   $$\frac{125 - 14}{35} = \frac{111}{35} \text{ or } 3\frac{6}{35}$$

7. $(11 + 34)^2$

8. B. $\frac{1}{52}$
   Solution:
   Total numbers of cards in a deck $= 52$
   King of Hearts in a deck $= 1$
   Probability of King of Hearts $= 1/52$

9. 1170m³
   Solution:
   Volume of rectangular block $=$ height x length x width
   $= 13 \times 15 \times 6 = 1170m^3$

10. B. 15 balls
    Solution:
    1st row: 1
    2nd row: 2
    3rd row: 3
    4th row: 4
    5th row: 5
    $1+2+3+4+5=15$

TEST 9 SOLUTION

1. 5 m
   Solution:
   Volume = length x width x height
   $50m^3 = 2m(x)(x)$
   $50m^3 = 2x^2$
   $x^2 = 50m^3/2m$
   $x^2 = 25m^2$
   $x = 5m$

2. A. 8179 square meters
   Solution:
   $24,537 \div 3 = 8179$

3. -720
   Solution:
   -954 – (-234)
   -954 + 234 = -720

4. B. 30 days
   Solution:
   $6 = 2 \times 3$
   $5 = \quad\quad\quad 5$
   $3 = \quad\quad 3$
   $2 = 2$
   _____
   LCM = $2 \times 3 \times 5 = 30$

5. B. $\frac{3}{8}$
   Solution: $\frac{p}{q}$ is a proper fraction
   when p < q

6. D. 30 meters
   Solution:
   Length of cloth bought later
   $20 \times 50\%$
   $20 \times 0.5 = 10$
   Total length of cloth be bought
   $20 + 10 = 30$

7. $2N + 5$

8. 10n
   Solution:
   $\frac{10 pancakes}{1\ box} = \frac{\#pancakes}{n}$
   #pancakes = 10n

9. A. 2.525L
   Solution:
   $250 + 375 + 500 + 400 =$
   1525mL
   $1525mL \div 1000 = 1.525L$
   $1.525L + 1L = 2.525L$

10. C. 90
    Solution:
    A right triangle always contains a 90-degree angle. So, the sum of the remaining angles is,
    180 – 90 = 90.
    There is no angle greater than 90-degree angle.

TEST 10 SOLUTION

1. 5.4 Km

   Solution:
   5,371.32 meters in kilometers is 5.37132 Km which is equal to 5.4 correct to once decimal place

2. A. 36 jackets

   Solution:
   Jackets sold; $9 \times 12 = 108$
   Jackets left,
   $144 - 108 = 36$

3. B. £39.31

   Solution:
   $51.67 - 12.36 = 39.31$

4. D. 75

   Solution:
   Total number of earrings must be divisible by 5.
   LCM of 4, 6, and 8 is 24
   The number of earrings must be divisible by 24 leaving 3 as remainder.
   Looking at the answer choices, the only option is 75 since it is divisible by 5 and;
   $24 \times 3 + 3 = 75$

5. A. $37\frac{1}{3}$ glasses of milk

   Solution:
   $5\frac{1}{3} \times 7 = \frac{3\times5+1}{3} \times 7$
   $\frac{16}{3} \times 7 = \frac{112}{3}$
   $\frac{112}{3} = 37\frac{1}{3}$

6. £625

   Solution:
   Perimeter of pentagon = 5m x 5 = 25m
   Cost of fence = 25m x £25/m = £625

7. B. $\frac{3}{8}$

   Solution:
   Total number of flowers,
   $9+15 = 24$
   $\frac{9}{24} = \frac{9\div3}{24\div3} = \frac{3}{8}$

8. $100a + 80o$

9. A. 4436 sec

   Solution:
   $1\times60\times60 + 13\times60 + 56 = 4436$

10. D. 90 degrees

    Solution:
    Sum of angles in a triangle is 180.
    Number of degrees per 1 ratio,
    $180 \div (1+2+3) = 30$
    $3 \times 30 = 90$

TEST 11 SOLUTION

1. D. 5

    Solution:

    Ten thousandths is $\frac{1}{10,000}$

    $5 \times \frac{1}{10,000} = 0.0005$

2. $x = 1$

    Solution:

    $2.5 = \frac{7+3+2+x+1+1}{6}$

    $2.5 = \frac{14+x}{6}$

    $14 + x = 6\,(2.5)$

    $x = 15 - 14 = 1$

3. A. 200 meters

    Solution:

    $2 \times (85 + 15) = 2 \times 100 = 200$

4. A. 23500 mm

    Solution:

    Perimeter of decagon = 2.35m x 10

    $= 23.5m = 23500mm$

5. C. 13

    Solution:

    $20\frac{3}{4} \div 1\frac{1}{2} = \frac{4\times20+3}{4} \div \frac{2\times1+1}{2}$

    $\frac{83}{4} \div \frac{3}{2} = \frac{83}{4} \times \frac{2}{3}$

    $\frac{166}{12} = 13\frac{5}{6}$

6. $\frac{8}{11}$

    Solution:

    $1 - \frac{3}{11} = \frac{8}{11}$

7. D. 88%

    Solution:

    Percentage of mistakes,

    $6 \div 50 = 0.12 = 12\%$

    Percentage of correct answers

    $100\% - 12\% = 88\%$

8. B. 12 cards

    Solution:

    $48 \div (3+5) = 6$

    Number of cards Jack received,

    $6 \times 3 = 18$

    Number of cards Rexell received,

    $6 \times 5 = 30$

    $30 - 18 = 12$

9. A. 325 km

    Solution:

    $\frac{1}{100} = \frac{3.25}{N}$

    $N = 3.25 \times 100 = 325$

10. C. $\frac{1}{13}$

    Solution:

    No. of Kings in a stack = 4

    Total No. of cards = 52

    So, probability of picking a King =

    $\frac{4}{52} = \frac{1}{13}$

TEST 12 SOLUTION

1. B. 69, 034, 035

   Solution:

   $69 \times 1,000,000 + 34 \times 1,000 + 35$

   $= 69,000,000 + 34,000 + 35$

   $= 69,034,035$

2. A. Harry

   Solution:

   Arranging the values in order, we get; 12, 23, 25

   The median or the middle value is 23 which is the amount paid by Harry.

3. A. £633.50

   Solution:

   Candies: $0.546 \times 1000 = 546$

   Chips: $0.75 \times 100 = 75$

   Chocolates: $1.25 \times 10 = 12.50$

   $546 + 75 + 12.5 = 633.50$

4. D. 2.5 cm

   Solution:

   Octagon has 8 equal sides

   Hence, 20cm/8 = 2.5cm side

5. $\frac{7}{4}$ or $1\frac{3}{4}$

   Solution:

   $9\frac{1}{4} - 7\frac{1}{2} = \frac{4 \times 9 + 1}{4} - \frac{2 \times 7 + 1}{2}$

   $\frac{37}{4} - \frac{15}{2} = \frac{37 - 30}{4}$

   $\frac{7}{4} = 1\frac{3}{4}$

6. B. 90 girls

   Solution:

   Number of boys,

   $150 \times 40\% = 60$

   Number of girls,

   $150 - 60 = 90$

7. A. 4:5

   Solution:

   Original number of oranges,

   $56 \div \frac{4}{5} = 70$

   $\frac{56}{70} = \frac{4}{5}$

8. D. 3200 square meters

   Solution:

   $\frac{1}{4} = \frac{10}{x}$; $x = 10 \times 4 = 40$

   $\frac{1}{4} = \frac{20}{y}$; $y = 20 \times 4 = 80$

   $40 \times 80 = 3200$

9. A. 16 bananas

   Solution:

   Number of bananas,

   $B = 2A$

   $2B + 3A = 56$

   $2 \times 2A + 3A = 56$

   $A = 8$

   $B = 2 \times 8 = 16$

10. C. 110 degrees

    Solution:

    $25 + 80 + 145 + N = 360$

    $N + 250 = 360$

    $N = 110$

TEST 13 SOLUTION

1. 420,000
   Solution:
   The number 416,928 rounded up
   to the nearest thousand would be
   420,000

2. D. -6
   Solution:
   Arrange from greatest to least
   4, -2, -6, -12, -34, -65
   The third highest number is -6

3. 40%
   Solution:
   $\frac{2}{5} = 2 \div 5 = 0.4$
   $0.4 \times 100\% = 40\%$

4. B. 18 meters
   Solution:
   Percentage used for pillowcases
   and bed covers,
   $5\% + 50\% = 55\%$
   Percentage used for curtain,
   $100\% - 55\% = 45\%$
   Length of cloth used for curtains
   $40 \times 45\% = 40 \times 0.45 = 18$
   meters

5. 24 candles
   Solution:
   Volume of box = 16 x 12 x 8 =
   1536cm^2
   Volume of one candle = 4x4x4 =
   64 cm^2
   No. of candles = 1536/64 = 24

6. D. 1350 pixels
   Solution:
   $1000 \times 1.35 = 1350$

7. $1000 - 50e$

8. A. £127
   Solution:
   1st day: 1
   2nd day: 2
   3rd day: 4
   4th day: 8
   5th day: 16
   6th day: 32
   7th day: 64
   $1+2+4+8+16+32+64 = 127$

9. B. 3000 grams
   Solution:
   $0.25 \times 12 = 3$ kg
   $3kg \times 1000 = 3000$

10. C. 3.375km
    Solution:
    $25 \times 135 = 3375m$
    $3375m \div 1000 = 3.375km$

TEST 14 SOLUTION

1. C. One million
    Solution:
    The actual balance is 546,745,
    which is more than half a million,
    hence the balance rounded off to
    nearest million would be 1 million

2. 6,400 km
    Solution:
    The hundreds place is 3
    The number on the right of 3 is 7
    which is greater than or equal to
    5.
    63|71 = 63+1|00
    Therefore, 6,400

3. A. £13.5
    Solution:
    Chocolates: 12×5.0 = 60
    Candies: 20×1.0 = 20
    Soda: 1×6.5 = 6.5
    Total cost= 60+20+6.5 = 86.5
    Money left: 100-86.5 = 13.5

4. C. 0.05 grams
    Solution:
    6.5÷ 130 = 0.05

5. C. 54 years old
    Solution:
    Two years from now, his age will
    be divisible by 8. This means that
    his current age when divided by 8
    will leave a remainder 8 – 2 = 6
    Amongst the answer choices, the
    only choice that fits is 54
    8 x 6 + 6 = 54

6. A. Improper fraction
    Solution:
    $\frac{P}{q}$ is a proper fraction if $p < q$
    Since $12 > 3$. Then, improper.

7. C. $2\pi^2$
    Solution:
    Area of circle $= \pi r^2$
    Given area $= \pi^3$
    So, $\pi r^2 = \pi^3$
    ---> $r = \pi$
    Now, perimeter of circle $= 2\pi r$
    As r$= \pi$, hence perimeter $= 2\pi^2$

8. 15%
    Solution:
    $3 \div 20 = 0.15$
    $0.15 \times 100\% = 15\%$

9. D. 2.4 meters
    Solution:
    $\frac{1.6}{2.8} = \frac{N}{4.2}$
    $N = \frac{1.6}{2.8} \times 4.2 = 2.4$

10. $N + N - 100$

TEST 15 SOLUTION

1. 2

   Solution:
   Hundred thousands is 100,000
   $2 \times 100{,}000 = 200{,}000$

2. D. $(3, 0)$

   Solution:
   The point $(1, 1)$, origin, and $(2, -1)$
   are either inside, or on the square.
   The point $(3, 0)$ is outside the
   square.

3. B. £275

   Solution:
   Let N be the amount he spent
   $500 - N \rightarrow$ pocket money
   $N + 50 \rightarrow$ pocket money
   $500 - N = N + 50$
   $N = 225$
   $500 - N = 500 - 225 = 275$

4. D. 18

   Solution:
   LCD is just the LCM of
   denominators.
   $3 = \quad 3$
   $9 = \quad 3 \times 3$
   $6 = \quad 3 \times \quad 2$
   LCD $= 3 \times 3 \times 2 = 18$

5. A. $\frac{17}{2}$ or $8\frac{1}{2}$

   Solution:
   $3 + \frac{4}{6} + 2 + \frac{3}{6} + 2\frac{2}{6}$
   $3 + 2 + 2 + \frac{4+3+2}{6} = 7 + \frac{9}{6}$
   $7 + 1\frac{3}{6} = 8\frac{1}{2}$

6. B. 12:13

   Solution:
   Length of another piece,
   $100 - 52 = 48$
   $\frac{48}{52} = \frac{48 \div 4}{52 \div 4} = \frac{12}{13}$
   $\frac{12}{13} = 12: 13$

7. $1000 - N$

8. D. 22 years old

   Solution:
   Age of Emma now,
   $2 \times 10 = 20$
   Age of Emma two years from now,
   $20 + 2 = 22$

9. C. 23 ducks

   Solution:
   Number of ducks
   $D = 3C - 10$
   Total number of legs
   $2D + 4C = 90$
   $2(3C-10) + 4C = 90$
   $6C - 20 + 4C = 90$
   $10C = 90 + 20$
   $10C = 110$
   $C = 11$
   $D = 3C - 10 = 3 \times 11 - 10 = 23$

10. A. 0.75km

   Solution:
   $500 \times 1.5 = 750$m
   750m $\div 1000 = 0.75$km

TEST 16 SOLUTION

1. -14, -13, -12, and -11

2. Twelve and five hundred forty three thousandth.

3. D. 82.212 meters
   Solution:
   $6.63 \times 12.4 = 82.212$

4. A. $6\frac{1}{4}$ kilometers
   Solution:
   $$2\frac{1}{2} \times 2\frac{1}{2}$$
   $$\frac{2 \times 2 + 1}{2} \times \frac{2 \times 2 + 1}{2}$$
   $$\frac{5}{2} \times \frac{5}{2} = \frac{25}{4} = 6\frac{1}{4}$$

5. C. £6300
   Solution:
   Bonus;
   $15{,}750 \times 60\%$
   $15{,}750 \times 0.6 = 9{,}450$
   Basic salary;
   $15{,}750 - 9{,}450 = 6300$

6. C. 7 yellow and 9 red beads
   Solution:
   $$\frac{yellow}{red} = \frac{49}{63}$$
   $$\frac{49}{63} = \frac{49 \div 7}{63 \div 7} = \frac{7}{9}$$

7. D. £40
   Solution:
   Overall cost,
   $$\frac{3}{5} = \frac{3 \times 12}{N}$$
   $N = 36 \times \frac{5}{3} = 60$
   Change,
   $100 - 60 = 40$

8. B. 14
   Solution:
   Total numbers $= 10$
   Average $= 7$
   Sum of 10 numbers $= 7 \times 10 = 70$
   A number 'x' is removed, and the average becomes 6:
   So, $6 = \frac{70 - x}{9} \rightarrow x = 14$

9. A. 51.47 kg
   Solution:
   Weight gained in kg,
   $4230g = 4.23kg$
   Total weight,
   $47.24 + 4.23 = 51.47kg$

10. A. 31.25m
    Solution:
    $5 \times 6.25 = 31.25m$

TEST 17 SOLUTION

1. Ten thousandths
   Solution:
   $$2 \times \frac{1}{10,000} = 0.0002$$
   $\frac{1}{10,000}$ is ten thousandths

2. B. 5 notebooks
   Solution:
   Remaining balance,

   $103 - 8 = 95$

   Number of notebooks bought,
   $95 \div 19 = 5$

3. 364
   Solution:
   $36472 \div 100 = 364.72$
   Therefore, 364

4. A. £58.40
   Solution:
   $524.15 - 465.75 = 58.40$

5. 1.925
   Solution:
   $25.125 (-23.2) = 1.925$

6. B. 33.33%
   Solution:
   $Cats = \frac{120}{360} \times 100 = 33.33\%$

7. A. 6
   Solution:
   $30 = 2 \times 3 \times 5$
   $42 = 2 \times 3 \times 7$
   $60 = 2 \times 2 \times 3 \times 5$
   $\overline{HCF = 2 \times 3}$
   $HCF = 6$

8. D. 225
   Solution:
   The square of a negative number
   is a positive.
   $(-15) \times (-15) = 225$

9. $\frac{15}{30}, \frac{20}{30}, \frac{24}{30}$
   Solution:
   The LCD of 2, 3, and 5 is 30
   $\frac{1}{2} = \frac{1}{2} \times \frac{15}{15} = \frac{15}{30}$
   $\frac{2}{3} = \frac{2}{3} \times \frac{10}{10} = \frac{20}{30}$
   $\frac{4}{5} = \frac{4}{5} \times \frac{6}{6} = \frac{24}{30}$

10. B. 55
    Solution:
    1: 1
    2: $1+0 = 1$
    3: $1+1 = 2$
    4: $2+1 = 3$
    5: $3+2 = 5$
    6: $5+3 = 8$
    7: $8+5 = 13$
    8: $13+8 = 21$
    9: $21+13 = 34$
    10: $34+21 = 55$

TEST 18 SOLUTION

1. 4

   Solution:

   Thousandths is $\frac{1}{1000}$

   $4 \times \frac{1}{1000} = 0.004$

2. C. 270 bacteria

   Solution:

   $10 \times 3 = 30$ (first hour)

   $30 \times 3 = 90$ (second hour)

   $90 \times 3 = 270$ (third hour)

3. A. 1250 apples

   Solution:

   One hour 40 min $= 60 + 40$

   $= 100$ minutes

   $125 \times 100 / 10 = 1250$

4. -45

   Solution:

   $135 \div (-3) = -45$

5. B. 54

   Solution:

   $18 = 2 \times 3 \times 3$

   $27 = \quad\ \ 3 \times 3 \times 3$

   LCM $= 2 \times 3 \times 3 \times 3$

   LCM $= 54$

6. 18 degrees

   Solution:

   Area of baseball sector $= 5\%$

   Angle of baseball sector $= 5\%$ x

   total angle of pie chart

   $= (5/100)$ x $360 = 18$ degrees

7. C. $\frac{3}{4}$

   Solution:

   $2\frac{1}{2} - 1\frac{3}{4} = \frac{2 \times 2 + 1}{2} - \frac{4 \times 1 + 3}{4}$

   $\frac{5}{2} - \frac{7}{4} = \frac{10}{4} - \frac{7}{4} = \frac{3}{4}$

8. A. £600

   Solution:

   $X - 5\%X = 570$

   $0.95X = 570$

   $X = 600$

9. C. 120 fruits

   Solution:

   Difference in ratio: $7-5 = 2$

   Every 1 ratio we have: $20 \div 2 = 10$

   Number of apples: $10 \times 5 = 50$

   Number of oranges: $10 \times 7 = 70$

   Total number of fruits: $50+70 = 120$

10. A. 10 shells

    Solution:

    Jermaine $= J$

    Jerry : $J/3$

    Jeremie: $2J/3$

    Total number of shells:

    $J+J/3+2J/3=30$

    $J = 15$

    Jeremie $= 2\left(\frac{1}{3} \times 15\right) = 10$

TEST 19 SOLUTION

1. 9
    Solution:
    Hundredths is $\frac{1}{100}$
    $9 \times \frac{1}{100} = 0.09$

2. A. 135
    Solution:
    Marks in Math = 35
    Marks in Science = 56
    Marks in English = 44
    $35+56+44 = 135$

3. B. £8000
    Solution:
    $100{,}000 \times 0.08 = 8000$

4. 15 students
    Solution:
    Students who speak at least 2
    languages also include those who
    speak all 3 languages. Hence, total
    number of such students =
    $4+4+5+2 = 15$

5. 20 students
    Solution:
    Referring to the Venn diagram,
    students who do not speak
    English are $= 5+2+6+7 = 20$

6. $\frac{3}{50}$

7. C. $\frac{20}{24}$
    Solution:
    $\frac{3}{4}$
    $\frac{12}{16} = \frac{12 \div 4}{16 \div 4} = \frac{3}{4}$
    $\frac{20}{24} = \frac{20 \div 4}{24 \div 4} = \frac{5}{6}$ →does not belong
    $\frac{21}{28} = \frac{21 \div 7}{287} = \frac{3}{4}$

8. C. £2100
    Solution:
    Let N be her original money
    $N - 75\%N = 525$
    $N - 0.75N = 525$
    $0.25N = 525$
    $N = 525 \div 0.25$
    $N = 2100$

9. A. 21 men
    Solution:
    Using inverse proportion,
    $\frac{12}{28} = \frac{16}{N}$
    $N = 16 \times \frac{28}{12} = 21$

10. B. 19 rabbits
    Solution:
    $55 = 3R-2$
    $55+2 = 3R$
    $57 = 3R$
    $R = 19$

TEST 20 SOLUTION

1. C. £13,700

   Solution:

   Rounding to nearest 100

2. B. £1575

   Solution:

   225 x 7 = 1575

3. D. 18

   Solution:

   $1000 \times 0.003 = 3$

   $100 \times 0.06 = 6$

   $10 \times 0.9 = 9$

   $3 + 6 + 9 = 18$

4. 1050

   Solution:

   $1000 \div 105 = 9$ remainder 55

   If we multiply 105 by 9, it will only give us three-digit number.

   Therefore, $105 \times 10 = 1050$

5. $\frac{6}{9}, \frac{4}{9}, \frac{3}{9}, \frac{1}{9}$

   Solution:

   Since the fractions are similar (common denominator).

   Then, arrange the numerator from highest to lowest

6. C. 2.5

   Solution:

   Median is the middle number of a data set. Since there are two middle numbers, i.e. 2 and 3, hence median is the average of these two numbers, which is 2.5

7. D. 150 people

   Solution:

   $\frac{men}{women} = \frac{4}{6} = \frac{60}{N}$

   $N = 60 \times \frac{6}{4} = 90$

   Total number of people

   $60 + 90 = 150$

8. J – 150

9. C. 144 voters

   Solution:

   Number of voters per 1 ratio,

   $270 \div (7+8) = 18$

   $18 \times 8 = 144$

10. B. 0.5 hours

    Solution:

    Total time,

    11min 10sec + 3min 36sec + 15min 14sec

    $(11 + 3 + 15)min = 29min$

    $(10 + 36 + 14)sec = 60sec = 1$ min

    $29min + 1 min = 30min$

    $30 \div 60 = 0.5$

TEST 21 SOLUTION

1. 0.354

   Solution:

   The thousands place is 3

   The number on the right of 3 is 8

   which is greater than or equal to 5

   0.353|87453 =

   0.353+0.001|00000

   Therefore, 0.354

2. B. 54L

   Solution:

   $50+4 = 54$

3. 395cm³

   Solution:

   Volume of juice box = 5x7x3=105

   Volume of milk carton = 5x10x10

   = 500 cm³

   So, answer = 500 – 105 = 395cm³

4. B. 5

   Solution:

   Using prime factorization

   $125 = 5 \times 5 \times 5$

   $125 = 5^3$

5. $\frac{11}{4}$

   Solution:

   $\frac{4 \times 2 + 3}{4} = \frac{11}{4}$

6. A. $\frac{25}{4}$ or $6\frac{1}{4}$

   Solution:

   $10 - 3\frac{6}{8} = 10 - \frac{8 \times 3 + 6}{8}$

   $\frac{80}{8} - \frac{30}{8} = \frac{50}{8} = \frac{25}{4}$

   $\frac{25}{4} = 6\frac{1}{4}$

7. B. 16%

   Solution:

   Percentage of correct answer,

   $(21 \div 25) \times 100\% = 84\%$

   Percentage of incorrect answer,

   $100\% - 84\% = 16\%$

8. D. £627

   Solution:

   $\frac{156.75}{5} = \frac{N}{20}$

   $N = \frac{156.75}{5} \times 20 = 627$

9. A. 5 meters

   Solution:

   $\frac{10}{6} = \frac{N}{3}$

   $N = \frac{10}{6} \times 3 = 5$

10. C. £180

    Solution:

    Money of Shakira,

    $S = J + 60$

    Sum of their money,

    $S + J = 300$

    $J + 60 + J = 300$

    $2J = 300 - 60$

    $2J = 240$

    $J = 120$

    $S = J + 60 = 120 + 60 = 180$

TEST 22 SOLUTION

1. A. 25.524km
   Solution:
   $25.294 + 0.23 = 25.524$

2. B. £40
   Solution:
   Total cost of sugar,
   $5 \times 12 = 60$
   Change,
   $100 - 60 = 40$

3. 85 degrees
   Solution:
   Sum of angles on a straight line = 180
   So, $y + 56 + 39 = 180$
   $y = 85$

4. C. -125
   Solution:
   $(-5)(-5)(-5)$
   $(25)(-5)$
   -125

5. $\frac{238}{15}$
   Solution:
   $5\frac{2}{3} \times 2\frac{4}{5}$
   $\frac{5 \times 3 + 2}{3} \times \frac{5 \times 2 + 4}{5}$
   $\frac{17}{3} \times \frac{14}{5}$
   $\frac{238}{15}$

6. $\frac{13}{5}$ or $2\frac{3}{5}$
   Solution:
   $2\frac{1}{2} - \frac{7}{10} = \frac{2 \times 2 + 1}{2} - \frac{7}{10} = \frac{18}{10}$
   $\frac{18}{10} + \frac{4}{5} = \frac{9 + 4}{5} = \frac{13}{5}$

7. A. £143571.42
   Solution:
   Let N be his money 3 years ago
   $N + 5\%N = 150750$
   $1.05N = 150750$
   $N = 143571.42$

8. A. 1:2
   Solution:
   1:2| $20 \div (1+2) = 6.666...$
   →fraction, impossible
   1:1| $20 \div (1+1) = 10$ → whole number, possible
   2:3| $20 \div (2+3) = 4$ → whole number, possible
   2:8| $20 \div (2+8) = 2$ → whole number, possible

9. A. 6 juice powders
   Solution:
   $\frac{1 \; juicepowder}{8 \; glasses \; of \; milk} = \frac{N}{48}$
   $N = 48 \div 8 = 6$

10. B. 23 kilograms
    Solution:
    Weight of Saira: $N + 5$
    $N + 5 + N = 41$
    $N = 18$
    $N + 5 = 18 + 5 = 23$

TEST 23 SOLUTION

1. C. 7 jackets
   Solution:
   Total money he received,
   $50 + 100 + 125 + 75 = 350$
   Number of jackets he can buy,
   $350 \div 50 = 7$

2. A. 1250 bills
   Solution:
   $125000 \div 100 = 1250$

3. A. 2180.71 yards
   Solution:
   $6542.13 \div 3 = 2180.71$

4. -14
   Solution:
   $-2.5 \times 4 = -10$
   $12 \div 3 = 4$
   $-10 - 4 = -14$

5. A. 216
   Solution:
   $LCM \times HCF = product$
   $LCM = 1296 \div 6$
   $LCM = 216$

6. C. Mixed number
   Solution:
   Whole number + fraction is a
   mixed number.

7. B. $387\frac{1}{2}$ meters
   Solution:
   $\frac{31}{4} \times 50 = \frac{1550}{4}$
   $387\frac{2}{4} = 387\frac{1}{2}$

8. $\frac{11}{15}$
   Solution:
   The LCD of 3 and 5 is 15
   $\frac{2}{3} \times \frac{5}{5} = \frac{10}{15}$
   $\frac{4}{5} \times \frac{3}{3} = \frac{12}{15}$
   $\frac{10}{15}, \frac{11}{15}, \frac{12}{15}$

9. A. $29\frac{2}{5}$ kilogram
   Solution:
   $40 - 10\frac{3}{5} = 40 - \frac{5 \times 10 + 3}{5}$
   $40 - \frac{53}{5} = \frac{200 - 53}{5}$
   $\frac{147}{5}$ or $29\frac{2}{5}$

10. C. 6 degrees
    Solution:
    The sum of angles of a triangle is
    180 degrees
    $x + 3x\text{-}2 + 50\text{-}x = 180$
    $3x + 48 = 180$
    $3x = 180\text{-}48$
    $3x = 132$
    $x = 44$
    $3x - 2 = 3 \times 44 - 2 = 130$
    $50 - x = 50 - 44 = 6 \rightarrow$ lowest

TEST 24 SOLUTION

1. C. £600

   Solution:
   Cost after buying,
   $6 \times 300 = 1800$
   Number of 3- jackets,
   $6 \times 12 = 72$
   $72 \div 3 = 24$
   Cost after re-selling,
   $24 \times 100 = 2400$
   Profit $= 2400 - 1800 = 600$

2. B. 114.1 minutes

   Solution:
   $3423 \div 30 = 114.1$

3. A. 75mL

   Solution:
   Amount of water reduced,
   $5 \times 5 = 25$
   Amount of remaining water,
   $100 - 25 = 75$

4. C. 40 slices

   Solution:
   $5 \div \frac{1}{8} = 5 \times 8 = 40$

5. $\frac{2}{11}$

   Solution:
   Since all numerators have the same value, then the smallest would we the highest value on the denominator.

6. $\frac{133}{60}$

   Solution:
   The LCD of 6,8 and 10 is 120
   $\frac{4}{6} = \frac{80}{120}; \frac{6}{8} = \frac{90}{120}; \frac{8}{10} = \frac{96}{120}$
   $\frac{80}{120} + \frac{90}{120} + \frac{96}{120} = \frac{266}{120}$
   $\frac{266}{120} = \frac{133}{60}$

7. A. 62.5%

   Solution:
   Total students $= 15 + 25 = 40$
   Percentage of girls:
   $25 \div 40 \times 100\% = 62.5\%$

8. D. £11500

   Solution:
   $10000 \times 15\% = 1500$
   Total monthly income:
   $10000 + 1500 = 11500$

9. D. $\frac{1}{12}$

   Solution:
   Probability of getting heads $= \frac{1}{2}$
   Probability of getting a six $= \frac{1}{6}$
   Combined probability $= \frac{1}{2} \times \frac{1}{6} = \frac{1}{12}$

10. D. 9 trees

    Solution:
    Jack planted: $J = \frac{R}{2} + 3$
    Total number of trees planted
    $J + R = 21$
    $\frac{R}{2} + 3 + R = 21$
    $R = 12$
    $J = \frac{12}{2} + 3 = 9$

TEST 25 SOLUTION

1. B. 5
    Solution:
    Let N be the original number.
    Her mistake,
    N × 9 = 405
    N = 45
    Correct answer,
    45 ÷ 9 = 5

2. A. £101.35
    Solution:
    351.85 − 250.50 = 101.35

3. A. 8 cubic meters
    Solution:
    Volume = s^3
    Volume = 2×2×2
    Volume = 8

4. $\frac{26}{7}$

    Solution:
    $\frac{(7×3+5)}{7} = \frac{26}{7}$

5. $\frac{1}{8}$

    Solution:
    $0.125 = 0.125 × \frac{1000}{1000} = \frac{125}{1000}$
    $\frac{125}{1000} = \frac{125÷125}{1000÷125} = \frac{1}{8}$

6. B. 3:7
    Solution:
    Number of absents,
    50-35 = 15
    $\frac{15}{35} = \frac{15÷5}{35÷5} = \frac{3}{7}$
    $\frac{3}{7} = 3:7$

7. B. 72 chocolates
    Solution:
    Number of chocolates per 1 ratio,
    45 ÷ 5 = 9
    Ivet's chocolates
    3×9 = 27
    All Chocolates
    45 + 27 = 72

8. (65+x/1000) kg

9. $\frac{8+n}{15+d}$

10. B. 21 blue beads
    Solution:
    Number of blue beads,
    B = 2R + 3
    Total number of beads,
    B + R = 30
    2R + 3 + R = 30
    3R + 3 = 30
    3R = 30 − 3
    3R = 27
    R = 27 ÷ 3
    R = 9
    B = 2×9 + 3
    B = 21

TEST 26 SOLUTION

1. B. 40 meters

   Solution:

   Pentagon has 5-sides,

   $200 \div 5 = 40$

2. $2 \times 3 \times 7 \times 11$

   Solution:

   462 is an even number so it is divisible by 2

   $462 \div 2 = 231$

   The sum of digit of 231 is divisible by 3 so it is divisible by 3

   $231 \div 3 = 77$

   $77 = 7 \times 11$

   Therefore, $2 \times 3 \times 7 \times 11$

3. A. 9 square meters

   Solution:

   $5^2 - 4^2$

   $25 - 16 = 9$

4. $3\frac{3}{7}$

   Solution:

   $24 \div 7 = 3$ remainder 3

   Therefore $3\frac{3}{7}$

5. A. $\frac{1}{2}$

   Solution:

   $\frac{3}{4} \times \frac{4}{5} \times \frac{5}{6} = \frac{60}{120}$

   $\frac{60 \div 60}{120 \div 60} = \frac{1}{2}$

6. B. $\frac{1}{3}$

   Solution:

   $\frac{6}{18} = \frac{6 \div 6}{18 \div 6} = \frac{1}{3}$

7. 3

   Solution:

   $\frac{1}{4} + \frac{3}{4} + \frac{8}{4} = \frac{1+3+8}{4}$

   $\frac{12}{4} = 3$

8. A. 3:5

   Solution:

   Number of boys,

   $32 - 20 = 12$

   $\frac{12}{20} = \frac{12 \div 4}{20 \div 4} = \frac{3}{5}$

   $\frac{3}{5} = 3 : 5$

9. D. 6 days

   Solution:

   3 dozen $= 36$

   $\frac{6 dresses}{1 day} = \frac{36}{N}$

   $N = 36 \div 6 = 6$

10. D. 696 glasses of water

    Solution:

    $N = 8 \times 29 \times 3 = 696$

TEST 27 SOLUTION

1. B. 45 meters
    Solution:
    Perimeter $= 12 + 18 + 15 = 45$m

2. $2 \times 2 \times 3 \times 3$
    Solution
    $36 \div 2 = 18$
    $18 \div 2 = 9$
    $9 \div 3 = 3$
    $3 \div 3 = 1$, therefore $2 \times 2 \times 3 \times 3$

3. A. £71
    Solution:
    $17.75 \div \frac{1}{4} = 17.75 \times 4 = 71$

4. $\frac{3}{20}$
    Solution:
    $\frac{3}{4} - \frac{3}{5}$
    The LCD of 4 and 5 is 20
    $\frac{3}{4} = \frac{15}{20}, \frac{3}{5} = \frac{12}{20}$
    $\frac{15}{20} - \frac{12}{20} = \frac{3}{20}$

5. $\frac{1}{3}$
    Solution:
    $1:3 = \frac{1}{3}$

6. A. 16 games
    Solution:
    Percentage of games won
    $= 100 - 20 = 80$
    $80\% \times 20$
    $0.8 \times 20 = 16$

7. C. 4:9
    Solution:
    Original area,
    $10 \times 12 = 120$
    Dimension of new area,
    $10 + 10 \times 50\% = 15$
    $12 + 12 \times 50\% = 18$
    New area
    $15 \times 18 = 270$
    $\frac{120}{270} = \frac{120 \div 30}{270 \div 30} = \frac{4}{9}$

8. D. £820
    Solution:
    $\frac{12300}{15} = 820$

9. C. £450
    Solution:
    Amount per 1 ratio,
    $150 \div 3 = 50$
    Largest amount
    $9 \times 50 = 450$

10. A. 10 lemons
    Solution:
    Let N be the original number of lemons
    $3N - 5 = 25$
    $3N = 25 + 5$
    $3N = 30$
    $N = 10$

TEST 28 SOLUTION

1. B. 72 meters
   Solution:
   A regular octagon has 8 equal sides,
   $8 \times 9 = 72$

2. A. 100
   Solution:
   $12+16+20+24+28 = 100$

3. $6\frac{2}{3}$

   Solution:
   $20 \div 3 = 6$ remainder 2
   Therefore $6\frac{2}{3}$

4. C. 60
   Solution:
   $50 \div \frac{5}{6} = 50 \times \frac{6}{5} = 60$

5. $\frac{53}{12}$ or $4\frac{5}{12}$

   Solution:
   $5 - \frac{7}{12} = \frac{5 \times 12 - 7}{12}$
   $\frac{60-7}{12} = \frac{53}{12} = 4\frac{5}{12}$

6. D. 16.67%
   Solution:
   $\frac{5}{6} = 5 \div 6 = 0.83333...$
   $0.83333 \times 100\% \approx 83.33\%$
   $100\% - 83.33\% = 16.67\%$

7. C. 33.33%
   Solution:
   $20 \div 60 = 0.3333...$
   $0.3333 \times 100\% \approx 33.33\%$

8. C. 77 beads
   Solution:
   Using ratio and proportion,
   $\frac{3}{8} = \frac{21}{Y}$
   $3Y = 8 \times 21$
   $3Y = 168$
   $Y = 168 \div 3$
   $Y = 56 \rightarrow$ yellow beads
   Total number of beads,
   $56 + 21 = 77$

9. B. 63 months old
   Solution:
   Let the niece be y months old;
   $5y/7 + 18 = y$
   $y = 63$

10. 40s – 35g

TEST 29 SOLUTION

1. A. £5400

    Solution:

    $180 \times 5 \times 6 = 5400$

2. B. 100

    Solution:

    $96 \div 10 = 9.6$

    We multiply 10 by either 9 or 10

    $10 \times 9 = 90$; $10 \times 10 = 100$

    100 is nearest to 96 than 90.

3. $\frac{3}{13}$

    Solution:

    $4\frac{1}{3} = \frac{3 \times 4 + 1}{3} = \frac{13}{3}$

    $1 \div \frac{13}{3} = \frac{3}{13}$

4. D. £126

    Solution:

    $12 \times 10\frac{1}{2} = 12 \times \frac{2 \times 10 + 1}{2}$

    $12 \times \frac{21}{2} = 126$

5. $\frac{152}{15}$ or $10\frac{2}{15}$

    Solution:

    $20\frac{4}{5} - 10\frac{2}{3} = \frac{312 - 160}{15}$

    $\frac{152}{15} = 10\frac{2}{15}$

6. A. 28 beads

    Solution:

    Number of beads she gave,

    $35 \times 20\% = 7$

    $35 - 7 = 28$

7. B. 3:10

    Solution:

    Let N be the no. of wrong answers

    $3N + 2 \rightarrow$ no. of correct answers

    $3N + 2 + N = 26$

    $N = 6$

    Number of correct answers

    $3N + 2 = 3 \times 6 + 2 = 20$

    $\frac{6}{20} = \frac{3}{10} = 3:10$

8. A. 7 oranges

    Solution:

    $\frac{30\ apples}{5\ mangoes} \times \frac{12\ mangoes}{3\ oranges} = \frac{24\ apples}{1\ orange}$

    $\frac{24}{1} = \frac{168}{N}$

    $N = 168 \div 24 = 7$

9. C. 72 candies

    Solution:

    Number of candies per 1 ratio,

    $432 \div (5+7) = 36$

    Monique's candies: $5 \times 36 = 180$

    Yves' candies: $7 \times 36 = 252$

    $252 - 180 = 72$

10. A. 15 and 20

    Solution:

    The hypotenuse is the longest side of the right triangle.

    Length of 1 ratio,

    $25 \div 5 = 5$

    Length of legs

    $3 \times 5 = 15$

    $4 \times 5 = 20$

TEST 30 SOLUTION

1. B. 2352

   Solution:

   $2345 \div 8 = 293$ remainder 1

   Therefore, $8 \times 294 = 2352$

2. $\frac{9}{20}$

   Solution:

   $\frac{3}{5} \times \frac{3}{4} = \frac{9}{20}$

3. $\frac{39}{4}$ or $9\frac{3}{4}$

   Solution:

   $15\frac{1}{4} - 5\frac{1}{2} = \frac{4 \times 15 + 1}{4} - \frac{2 \times 5 + 1}{2}$

   $\frac{61}{4} - \frac{11}{2} = \frac{61 - 22}{4}$

   $\frac{39}{4}$ or $9\frac{3}{4}$

4. A. 342 mangoes

   Solution:

   To his neighbor: $400 \times 5\% = 20$

   Remaining mangoes: $400 - 20 = 380$

   Eaten by family: $380 \times 10\% = 38$

   $380 - 38 = 342$

5. A. 35%

   Solution:

   Percentage of girls,

   $52 \div 80 = 0.65$

   $0.65 \times 100\% = 65\%$

   Percentage of boys

   $100\% - 65\% = 35\%$

6. C. £378

   Solution:

   Annie's money: $210 \times 80\% = 168$

   $210 + 168 = 378$

7. D. 72

   Solution:

   Fraction of boys,

   $1 - \frac{5}{8} = \frac{3}{8}$

   $\frac{3}{8} = \frac{N}{192}$

   $N = \frac{3}{8} \times 192 = 72$

8. B. 48 feet

   Solution:

   Length per 1 ratio: $20 \div 5 = 4$

   Length per piece,

   $3 \times 4 = 12$; $4 \times 4 = 16$; $5 \times 4 = 20$

   Total length

   $12 + 16 + 20 = 48$

9. A. 45:8

   Solution:

   $\frac{15\ apples}{8\ mangoes} \times \frac{12\ mangoes}{4\ oranges} = \frac{45}{8}$

10. C. 60 meters

    Solution:

    Length of 1 ratio,

    $10 \div 5 = 2$

    Length of other sides,

    $12 \times 2 = 24$; $13 \times 2 = 26$

    Perimeter of triangle,

    $10 + 24 + 26 = 60$

TEST 31 SOLUTION

1. C. 52 cm
   Solution:
   $63 \times \frac{1}{3} = 21$
   $63-21=42$
   $42+10 = 52$

2. James
   Solution:
   James' height in cm
   $= 60 \times 2.54$
   $= 152.4$

3. £6.50 per box and 7
   7 pens per box
   Solution:
   $52 \div 8 = 6.50$
   $56 \div 8 = 7$

4. A. 3
   Solution:
   $-4 \times (-4) + 2 \times (-4) -k(-4) – 20 = 0$
   $16-8+4k-20=0$
   $k=3$

5. B. 3:4
   Solution:
   Number of boys,
   $56-32=24$
   $24:32 = 3:4$

6. 1.35 kg
   Solution:
   $0.135 \times 10 = 1.35$

7. B. 18
   Solution:
   $90 = \mathbf{2} \times \mathbf{3} \times \mathbf{3} \times 5$
   $72 = \mathbf{2} \times 2 \times 2 \times \mathbf{3} \times \mathbf{3}$
   HCF$= 2 \times 3 \times 3 = 18$

8. C. 12 pages
   Solution:
   30 mins $= 0.5$ hr
   $2 \div \frac{1}{12} = 24$ pages per hour
   $24 \times 0.5 = 12$

9. 651.05 kg
   Solution:
   $13.021 \times 50 = 651.05$ kg

10. C. School
    Solution:
    10.16 min is the least among them

TEST 32 SOLUTION

1. C. 183.77 minutes
   Solution:
   183.76|5
   183.77

2. D. 16 hours and 15 minutes
   Solution:
   Convert to 24hr time
   6:30am = 6 hrs and 30 mins
   10:45pm = 22 hrs and 45 mins
   22 hrs 45 mins - 6 hrs 30 mins
   16 hrs and 15 mins

3. W=12.5 cm
   L=17.5 cm
   Solution:
   L = W+5
   P=2×(L+W)
   60 = 2×(W+5 + W)
   30=2W+5
   W=12.5
   L=12.5+5=17.5

4. B. ten millions

5. C. 24 in
   Solution:
   Vol. of first box
   6×4×27=648
   Vol. of second box
   648×2 = 1296
   1296=9×6×H
   H=24

6. 4916
   Solution:
   49|61=5000
   49|16=4900

7. A. $1\frac{3}{5}$ hours
   Solution:
   $8 \times \frac{1}{5} = \frac{8}{5}$ or $1\frac{3}{5}$

8. £(4.5b-2)
   Solution:
   b×25%=0.25b
   b-0.25b=0.75b
   0.75b×6-2=4.5b-2

9. 1.5 kiloliters/hr
   Solution:
   $25\frac{liters}{minute} \times \frac{1}{1000}\frac{kiloliters}{liters} \times 60\frac{min}{hr}$
   =1.5

10. 144°
    Soltion:
    Let N be the sum of two angles
    Let M be the third angle
    N =4M
    N+M=180
    4M+M=180
    M=36
    N=4×36=144

TEST 33 SOLUTION

1. D. 1759
   Solution:
   $1|759 = 2000$

2. 24 days
   Solution:
   $8 = 2 \times 2 \times 2$
   $12 = 2 \times 2 \times 3$
   $LCM = 2 \times 2 \times 2 \times 3 = 24$

3. A. 546
   Solution:
   All choices have tens digit less than 5
   A, B, and C are divisible by 3 and 7
   Only A has ones digit greater than hundreds digit

4. D. 6
   Solution:
   $18 = \mathbf{2} \times \mathbf{3} \times 3$
   $12 = \mathbf{2} \times 2 \times \mathbf{3}$
   $24 = \mathbf{2} \times 2 \times 2 \times \mathbf{3}$
   $HCF = 2 \times 3 = 6$

5. £224.75
   Solution:
   $250 \div 10 = 25$
   $25 \times 8.99 = 224.75$

6. A. 13224
   Solution:
   $1.45 \text{ hrs} \times 60 = 87 \text{ mins}$
   $1216 \div 8 = 152 \text{ words per min}$
   $152 \times 87 = 13224$

7. A. 9th day
   Solution:
   $24 + 6N - 4N/4 = 70$
   $N = 9.2 \text{ or } 9 \text{ days}$

8. B. 125 cm2
   Solution:
   $2 + 1 = 3$
   $60 \div 3 = 20$
   $2 \times 20 : 1 \times 20 = 40 : 20$
   $40 \div 4 = 10$
   $A_1 = 10 \times 10 = 100$
   $20 \div 4 = 5$
   $A_2 = 5 \times 5 = 25$
   $100 + 25 = 125$

9. A. 12
   Solution:
   $3 \times 3 = 9$
   $12 \times 9 = 1080$
   $1080 \div 9 = 12$

10. B. £103.90
    Solution:
    $6 \times 5.50 = 33$
    $136.90 - 33 = 103.90$

TEST 34 SOLUTION

1. B. 21

   Solution:
   Choices C and D are both greater than 33
   84 is not divisible by Choice A
   Therefore, B

2. B. £310

   Solution:
   12.40×25=310

3. D. 22 cm

   Solution:

6	X
8	24

   Perimeter 6:
   6=2×(L+W)
   L+W=3
   W=1 ; L=2
   Perimeter 8:
   8=2×(L+W)
   L+W=4
   W=1 ; L=3
   Perimeter 24
   24=2×(L+W)
   L+W=12
   W=3 ; L=9
   Therefore Perimeter X has
   L=9 and W=2
   P=2×(9+2)=22

4. Wednesday

   Solution:
   2.5>2.15>2.0

5. B. 3:4

   Solution:
   12:16 = 3:4

6. A. 225

   Solution:
   8%×N=18
   N=225

7. B. 6

   Solution:
   8×1/4=2
   8-2=6

8. £168 bag
   £56 dress
   Solution:
   Let B be the cost of a bag
   Let D be the cost of a dress
   B = 3D
   B+D=224
   3D+D=224
   D=56
   B=3×56=168

9. Ali

   Solution:
   Lily = 13×5+16×50=865
   Ali = 3×5 + 21×50 = 1065

10. D. 13

    Solution:
    12 + p + p+5 = 33
    p=8
    p+5 = 8+5 = 13

TEST 35 SOLUTION

1. 0.03 kg
   Solution:
   $237.325g = 0.237325kg$
   $0.237325 \div 8 = 0.029665625$
   $0.02|9665625 = 0.03$

2. B. 210 days
   Solution:
   $30 = 2 \times 3 \times 5$
   $7 = 7$
   $LCM = 2 \times 3 \times 5 \times 7 = 210$

3. A. 6260
   Solution:
   $625|8 = 6260$

4. D. 8
   Solution:
   LCM × HCF
   = product of two numbers
   Hence; $24 \times 4 = m \times 12$
   $m = 8$

5. 20
   Solution:
   $N + N+1 + N+2 = 57$
   $N = 18$
   $N+2 = 18+2 = 20$

6. B. $(3, 0)$
   Solution:
   For a point to be located on the x-axis, the y-coordinate of that point should be equal to zero. Hence, the only point that fulfills this condition is $(3, 0)$

7. A. 27
   Solution:
   $4X+3X=21$
   $7X=21$
   $X=3$
   $Y+Y+Y+Y=36$
   $4Y=36$
   $Y=9$
   $X \times Y = 3 \times 9 = 27$

8. B. 38.10
   Solution:
   $15-1 = 14$
   $14 \times 2.40 + 4.5 = 38.10$

9. A. £71.25
   Solution:
   $60 \times \frac{3}{16} = 11.25$
   $60+11.25 = 71.25$

10. 3.2 liters
    Solution:
    $\frac{1}{8}N+2 = \frac{3}{4}N$
    $\left(\frac{3}{4} - \frac{1}{8}\right)N = 2$
    $N = 3.2$

TEST 36 SOLUTION

1. 96 in²
   Solution:
   P=2×(L+W)
   40=2×(L+8)
   L=12
   A=L×W=12×8=96

2. B. 35%
   Solution:
   There are 20 triangles
   7 of them are shaded
   $\frac{7}{20}×100\% = 35\%$

3. D. 18
   Solution:
   $\frac{3}{4}×8 = 6$
   $6÷\frac{1}{3}=18$

4. A. 40
   Solution:
   Back solving,
   15×12 = 180
   180÷4=45
   45-5=40

5. D. 5:9
   Solution:
   48 = N-12
   N=60
   60:(60+48) = 60:108
   5:9

6. $1\frac{7}{15}$ hours
   Solution:
   $\frac{2}{3}+\frac{4}{5}=\frac{10+12}{15} = \frac{22}{15}$ or $1\frac{7}{15}$

7. B. £12.30
   Solution:
   100-7N = 13.90
   7N = 100-13.90
   N=12.30

8. D. A(-4,4) B(4,-4)
   Solution:
   Point A is to the left and above of
   origin, hence coordinates of point
   A are (negative, positive)
   Point B is right and below of
   origin, hence coordinates of point
   B are (positive, negative), hence
   option 'D' is the correct answer

9. Rose
   Solution:
   Rose' error: 192.83-190=2.83
   Gavin's error: 192.83-186 = 6.83
   Since 2.83<6.83, therefore Rose is
   more accurate

10. C. 5
    Solution:
    $\frac{7+3+5+2+8}{5} = \frac{25}{5} = 5$

TEST 37 SOLUTION

1. D. 24
    Solution:
    No. of customers who bought 5 muffins
    42-10-8-7-9=8
    Ordered at least 3 muffins.
    7+9+8=24

2. B. 0.0483 cm
    Solution:
    483÷1000=0.483
    0.483÷10=0.0483

3. £1075
    Solution:
    1000÷2=500
    500×2.15=1075

4. A. 11:30 am
    Solution:
    Convert to 24-hour time
    1:15= 13hr 15min
    13hr 15min−1hr 45min=11hr 30min
    Therefore 11:30am

5. D. 72
    Solution:
    18×10=180
    $180×\frac{3}{5}=108$
    180-108=72

6. 3×3×13×17
    Solution:
    1989÷3=663
    663÷3=221
    221×13=17
    17÷17=1
    3×3×13×17

7. C. 21L
    Solution:
    S=L
    M=3S
    0.25×S + 0.50×M + 0.75×L = 35
    0.25×S+0.50×(3×S)+0.75×S=35
    S = 14
    M=3×14=42
    42×0.5=21L

8. £400
    Solution:
    Commission = 100 −35−25 = 40%
    Commission amount = £1000 x$\frac{40}{100}$
    = £400

9. B. 6
    Solution:
    3 x 800 = 2400g = 2.4 kg
    2.4/0.4 = 6

10. A. 49π cm²
    Solution:
    r=D/2=14÷2=7
    A=π ×r²
    A=π ×7×7
    A=49π cm²

TEST 38 SOLUTION

1. A. 0.21 kg
    Solution:
    10×cube = 6×cylinder
    10×cube = 6×0.35
    Cube = 0.21

2. B. 5:45 p.m
    Solution:
    15:15 = 15hrs 15mins
    15hrs 15mins + 2hrs 30mins
    17hrs 45mins – 12hrs 00min
    5:45 pm

3. 5 meters
    Solution:
    A = 24×15 = 360
    L= 24-6 = 18
    360÷18=20
    20-15 = 5

4. D. 26
    Solution:
    We need to add all the numbers that are shown in overlapped portions, including the overlapping by all three circles.
    So, the answer is: 10+7+3+6 = 26

5. A. 25%
    Solution:
    100-80=20
    $\frac{20}{80}$×100%=25%

6. 10 cm
    Solution:
    Length of pencil = 16 cm
    Length of eraser = 6 cm
    16-6=10

7. B. -46
    Solution:
    -46 < -17 < -3 < 0

8. D. £90
    Solution:
    Cost of pears: 33÷3 = 11
    Cost of avocado: 60÷5 = 12
    11×6 + 12×2 = 90

9. A. 96
    Solution:
    $12÷\frac{1}{4}$=48
    48×2 = 96

10. C. 8
    Solution:
    32×4=128
    128÷16 = 8

TEST 39 SOLUTION

1. B. 40°
   Solution:
   $\angle KOL + \angle LON = 180^o$
   $\angle KOL + 90^o = 180^o$
   $\angle KOL = 90^o$
   $\angle JON = \angle KOM = 130^o$
   $\angle KOM = \angle KOL + \angle LOM$
   $\angle LOM = 130 - 90 = 40^o$

2. D. Both A and B
   Solution:
   13 and 19 both occur three times in the given data set, hence both of them are the mode of the given data set

3. A. Darren
   Solution:
   Darren: $8\frac{8}{15} = \frac{1536}{180}$
   Steve: $\frac{207}{30} = \frac{1242}{180}$
   Anthony: $\frac{139}{18} = \frac{1390}{180}$
   $\frac{1536}{180} > \frac{1390}{180} > \frac{1242}{180}$
   Therefore, Darren cycled the farthest

4. 40%
   Solution:
   $\frac{14}{35} \times 100\% = 40\%$

5. D. 187.50 grams
   Solution:
   4:3 = 250:N
   N=250×3÷4 = 187.50

6. C. 56 years old
   Solution:
   Peter's age = 3×7 = 21
   Mother's age = 2×(21+7)=56

7. B. Acute angle
   Solution:

8. 329 coins
   Solution:
   65.80×100 = 6580
   6580÷20 = 329

9. 9 boxes
   Solution:
   4+1=5
   45÷5=9

10. B. 22.5L
    Solution:
    6×15=90cans
    90×0.25 = 22.5L

TEST 40 SOLUTION

1. C. 4 thousandths

2. 102 cupcakes
   Solution:

    $=16$

   $=2$

   $16 \times 6 + 2 \times 3 = 102$

3. D. £33.15
   Solution:
   $6 \times 6 + 3 = 39$
   $39 \times 0.85 = 33.15$

4. A. 80
   Solution:
   Arrange from smallest to greatest
   $\{69, 70, 73, 77, 78, 82, 85, 85, 90, 93\}$
   Then get the average of the middle two numbers
   $(78 + 82) \div 2 = 80$

5. 100
   Solution:
   $85+77+93+85+90+70+73+82 +78+69=802$
   $11 \times 82 = 902$
   $902 - 802 = 100$

6. C. -18 and -13

7. $(2m - 5) \div 3$
   Solution:
   $m + m = 2m$
   $2m + 6 - 11 = 2m - 5$
   $(2m - 5) \div 3$

8. C. -31
   Solution:
   $-627 < -235 < -89 < -31$

9. B. 12 sheets
   Solution:
   $3x - 15 \times \frac{1}{20}(3x) = 60$
   $3x - \frac{9}{4}x = 60$
   $x = 80$
   She gave $80 \times 3 \times \frac{1}{20} = 12$ sheets

10. -13
    Solution:
    $-36 = 15 \times 5 - 4 \times 5 + 7k$
    $-36 = 55 + 7k$
    $7k = -91$
    $k = -13$

TEST 41 SOLUTION

1. D. $\frac{1}{12}$

Solution:

The total number of outcomes for rolling two dices is 36. The favorable outcomes (which give a sum greater than 10) are only 3. i.e. (5,6), (6,5), (6,6). So, our required probability $= \frac{3}{36} = \frac{1}{12}$

2. $\frac{3}{5}$

Solution:
$$\frac{36min}{1\ hour} = \frac{36min}{60min} = \frac{3}{5}$$

3. B. 32 apples
   Solution:
   $192 \div 6 = 32$

4. £175
   Solution:
   Increase $= 25\% \times 140$
   Increase $= 35$
   Present Price $= 140+35 = 175$

5. A. 60 days
   Solution:
   $$\frac{18\ dolls}{8\ days} = \frac{135\ dolls}{n\ days}$$
   $$n = \frac{135 \times 8}{18} = 60$$

6. C. 4 days
   Solution:
   $1L = 1000mL$
   $$\frac{250mL}{1\ day} = \frac{1000mL}{n\ days}$$
   $$n = \frac{1000}{250} = 4$$

7. A. £12600
   Solution:
   $A = 24m \times 15m = 360\ m^2$
   £35 × 360 = 12600

8. 72 meters
   Solution:
   Perimeter of octagon $= 8 \times 36 = 288m$
   P of octagon = P of square
   $288 = 4 \times s$
   $s = 288 \div 4 = 72$

9. D. 92.4
   Solution:
   $$\frac{89+97+95+86+95}{5} = 92.4$$

10. 80,000 cubic centimeters
    Solution:
    $V = 80 \times 40 \times 25 = 80000$

TEST 42 SOLUTION

1. A. 87
   Solution:
   $4 = 2 \times 2$
   $6 = \quad 2 \times 3$
   $7 = \qquad 7$
   LCM$= 2 \times 2 \times 3 \times 7 = 84$
   $84 + 3 = 87$

2. 144 cubic meters
   Solution:
   $V = 8 \times 6 \times 3 = 144$

3. B. 597.7 km
   Solution:
   $0.8 + 5.2 + 60 + 524.5 + 8.2 = 597.7$

4. Hundred thousands

5. $9\frac{1}{12}$ kg
   Solution:
   $45\frac{3}{4} - 36\frac{2}{3} = (45 - 36) + \left(\frac{3}{4} - \frac{2}{3}\right)$
   $9 + \frac{9-8}{12} = 9\frac{1}{12}$

6. 40%
   Solution:
   $\frac{260 \: mangoes}{195+260+130+65} \times 100\% = 40\%$

7. C. 33.33%
   Solution:
   $\frac{480-320}{480} \times 100\% = 33.33\%$

8. (1, -4)
   Solution:
   $(-3+4, 4-8) = (1, -4)$

9. A. 1250 meters
   Solution:

   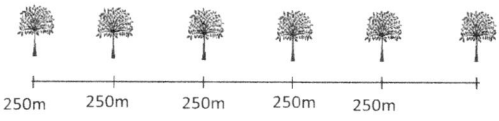

   $250 \times (6\text{-}1) = 1250$

10. B. 77.5 kph
    Solution:
    $12min \times \frac{1hour}{60min} = \frac{1}{5}hr$
    $15\frac{1}{2} \div \frac{1}{5} = 77.5$

TEST 43 SOLUTION

1. 54°
   Solution:
   Vertex angle + 2×base angle = 180
   180 – 2×63 = 54

2. 0.525
   Solution:
   420÷800 = 0.525

3. 3500 people
   Solution:
   25000×14% = 3500

4. D. 176.65m
   Solution:
   P = 24.5+65.23+12.05+65.3+9.57
   P = 176.65

5. D. £36
   Solution:
   12 dozen = 144 eggs
   144×0.50 = 72
   144×0.75 = 108
   108-72 = 36

6. A. 10m
   Solution:
   N + (3N+1) = 13
   4N + 1 = 13
   N = 3
   3N+1 = 3×3+1 = 10

7. B. £29.50
   Solution:
   1 set of meal = 12+8+3.5 = 23.50
   3 set of meals = 3×23.50 = 70.50
   100-70.50 = 29.50

8. 2,300,000

9. C. 85 wishes
   13600÷160 = 85

10. 2hrs 35min 45sec
    Solution:
    9345÷3600 = 2 remainder 2145
    2145÷60 = 35 remainder 45
    Therefore, 2hrs 35min 45sec

TEST 44 SOLUTION

1. 180 cubic meters
   Solution:
   $5 \times 12 \times 3 = 180$

2. C. £7797.85
   Solution:
   $6400 + 1250.50 + 500 - 352.65 = 7797.85$

3. A. 27.1 °C
   Solution:
   $$\frac{27.5 + 26.5 + 27 + 27.35 + 27.15}{5} = 27.1$$

4. 769,455.15

5. C. 27.5%
   Solution:
   1hr 15min + 2hr 45min + 3hr 15min
   = 7hr 15min or 7.15hrs
   10-7.15 = 2.75
   $\frac{2.75}{10} \times 100\% = 27.5\%$

6. 2.25m
   Solution:
   $V = L \times W \times H$
   $45 = 5 \times 4 \times H$
   $H = 2.25$

7. 8 students
   Solution:

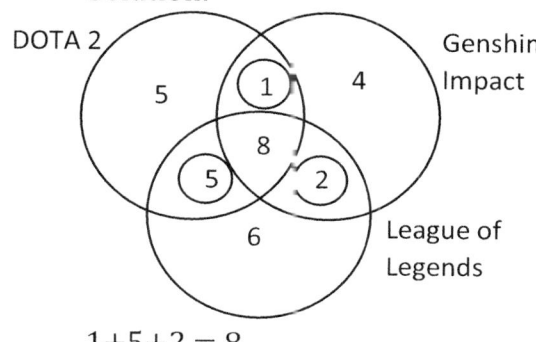

   $1 + 5 + 2 = 8$

8. A. £116,750
   Solution:
   $800000 = 120,000 + 563,250 + N$
   $N = 116,750$

9. D. £95
   Solution:
   Cost of 1 box: $2 \times 20 + 0.25 \times 30 = 47.5$
   Cost of 2 box: $2 \times 47.5 = 95$

10. -18
    Solution:
    $3N + 5 = 2(N-2)$
    $3N + 5 = 2N - 4$
    $N = -9$
    $2N = 2 \times -9 = -18$

TEST 45 SOLUTION

1. D. 514 minutes
   Solution:
   $5 \times 24 \times 60 + 2 \times 60 + 36 = 7356$
   $4 \times 24 \times 60 + 18 \times 60 + 2 = 6842$
   $7356 - 6842 = 514$

2. B. 1935 liters
   Solution:
   $15\text{min} \times 60 = 900\text{sec}$
   $2.15 \times 900 = 1935$

3. A. 213.5 km
   Solution:
   $45\frac{3}{4} \times 4\frac{2}{3} = \frac{183}{4} \times \frac{14}{3}$
   $= \frac{2562}{12} = 213.5$

4. 780
   Solution:
   $12 = 2 \times 2 \times 3$
   $13 = 13$
   $15 = 3 \times 5$
   $\text{LCM} = 2 \times 2 \times 3 \times 5 \times 13$
   $\text{LCM} = 780$

5. 100 jumps
   Solution:
   $150 \times 1\frac{1}{2} = 150 \div 1.5 = 100$

6. C. 5
   Solution:
   Arrange from lowest to highest.
   2,2,3,3,3,4,5,5,5,5,5
   5 appeared more frequently than
   the others.

7. 24.21 meters
   Solution:
   $2.69 \times 9 = 24.21$

8. Jerry
   Solution:
   $\frac{12}{17} = \frac{24}{34} > \frac{23}{34}$

9. D. $26007
   Solution:
   $155 \times 100 + 564 \times 10 + 4867 \times 1 = 26007$

10. 11.2 meters
    Solution:
    $\frac{5}{2.5} = \frac{N}{5.6}$
    $N = \frac{5}{2.5} \times 5.6 = 11.2$

TEST 46 SOLUTION

1. B. 98
   Solution:
   $88 \times 4 = 352$
   $90 \times 5 = 450$
   450-352 = 98

2. 1536
   Solution:
   6th day $= 192 \times 2 = 384$
   7th day $= 384 \times 2 = 768$
   8th day $= 768 \times 2 = 1536$

3. 1060 leaves
   Solution:
   $6 \div 1.2 = 5$
   $212 \times 5 = 1060$

4. C. 84 grams
   Solution:
   $7 \times 50 \times 0.24 = 84$

5. 6000 square centimeters
   Solution:
   $6 \times 50 \times 20 = 6000$

6. 5

7. A. 15 meals
   Solution:
   $$\frac{4 dog}{4 meal} \times 4 min = \frac{1 dog}{N \ meal} \times 60 min$$
   $N = 15$

8. 9.81

9. A. 20 necklaces
   Solution:
   $25 \div 1.25 = 20$

10. D. 9.81 cm
    Solution:
    $1cm : 2500 = N : 24525$
    $N = 9.81$

TEST 47 SOLUTION

1. 784 arrows
   Solution:
   $15 \times 28 = 420$
   $13 \times 28 = 364$
   $420 + 364 = 784$

2. C. 864 square meters
   Solution:
   $12 \times 12 = 144$
   $144 \times 6 = 864$

3. 600 eggs
   Solution:
   1 month = 4 weeks
   $4 \times 3 \times 50 = 600$

4. A. 2:00 PM
   Solution:
   $45 = \qquad 3 \times 3 \times 5$
   $60 = 2 \times 2 \times 3 \quad \times 5$
   LCM $= 2 \times 2 \times 3 \times 3 \times 5 = 180$
   180min = 3hrs
   11:00AM + 3hrs = 2:00PM

5. 190 L
   Solution:
   $\frac{N-76}{N} = \frac{3}{5}$
   $N - 76 = \frac{3}{5}N$
   $N - \frac{3}{5}N = 76$
   $\frac{2}{5}N = 76$
   $N = 190$

6. 34
   Solution:
   A 6-sided die has 3pairs of opposite faces
   $16+8+6+28+26+18 = 102$
   $102 \div 3 = 34$

7. D. 30 meters
   Solution:

   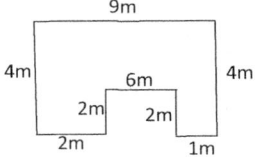

   $P = 4+9+4+1+2+6+2+2$
   $P = 30$

8. 0.0335 m
   Solution:
   $5.6835 - 5.65 = 0.0335$

9. A. £102.50
   Solution:
   $35.50 \times 2 + 25.50 \times 3 = 147.50$
   $250 - 147.50 = 102.50$

10. B. 35 minutes
    Solution:
    150:1 = 5250:N
    $N = 5250 \div 150 = 35$

TEST 48 SOLUTION

1. C. £68940.90
   Solution:
   $63.54 \times 155 = 9848.70$
   $9848.70 \times 7 = 68940.90$

2. A. $\frac{37}{108}$
   Solution:
   $$A + \left(A - \frac{1}{12}\right) + \left(A + \frac{1}{18}\right) = 1$$
   $$A = \frac{37}{108}$$

3. 6 days
   Solution:
   $12 \times 5 = 60$
   $60 \div 10 = 6$

4. D. 2125 liters
   Solution:
   $1 \times 60 + 25 = 85$
   $25 \times 85 = 2125$

5. 1800000 turns
   Solution:
   $1hr \times 60 \times 60 = 3600$
   $3600 \times 500 = 1800000$

6. 15%
   Solution:
   $$\frac{3}{2+3+4+5+6} \times 100\% = 15\%$$

7. $\frac{1}{6}$
   Solution:
   No. of possible outcomes $= 6 \times 6 = 36$
   List of outcomes with sum of 7
   $1+6, 2+5, 3+4, 4+3, 5+2, 6+1$
   $\frac{6}{36} = \frac{1}{6}$

8. 168 units
   Solution:
   $56 \times 3 = 168$

9. A. $1\frac{1}{2}$ cup
   Solution:
   $\frac{3}{8} : 4 = N : 16$
   $$N = \frac{\left(\frac{3}{8}\right)}{4} \times 16 = \frac{3}{2} \ or \ 1\frac{1}{2}$$

10. A. 247.5 kW
    Solution:
    $35+12+8=55$
    $55 \times 4.5 = 247.5$

TEST 49 SOLUTION

1. 150 oranges
   Solution:
   $120 \times 25\% = 30$
   $120 + 30 = 150$

2. 80
   Solution:
   $4 \times 5 = 20$
   $0.5 \times 0.5 = 0.25$
   $20 \div 0.25 = 80$

3. A. £11,165
   Solution:
   $18500 \times 9\% = 1665$
   $18500 + 1665 = 20165$
   $20165 - 9000 = 11165$

4. B. 84cm
   Solution:

   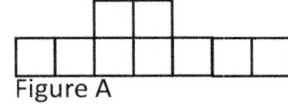
   Figure A   Figure B

   Since there are 18 equal sides
   making up the perimeter;
   $108 = 18s$
   $s = 6$
   Perimeter B $= 14s$
   Perimeter B $= 14 \times 6 = 84$

5. B. 75%
   Solution:
   $\frac{3.75}{5} \times 100\% = 75\%$

6. $7 \times 10{,}000 + 6 \times 1{,}000 + 2 \times 100 + 9 \times 10 + 4$

7. £90000
   Solution:
   $5000 \times 18 = 90000$

8. D. 25 targets
   Solution:
   $125 \times 20\% = 25$

9. 119 students
   Solution:
   $76 + 25 + 18 = 119$

10. D. 12.75 square meters
    Solution:
    $5 \times 5 - 3.5 \times 3.5$
    $25 - 12.25 = 12.75$

TEST 50 SOLUTION

1. B. £40
   Solution:
   $5.0 \times 1 + 14.5 \times 2 + 3.6 \times 5 + 2.5 \times 2$
   $+ 3.0 \times 1$
   $= 60$
   $100 - 60 = 40$

2. A. 585 successful shots
   Solution:
   $650 \times 90\% = 585$

3. 6hrs 5min 19sec
   Solution:
   3hr 52min 36sec + 2hr 12min
   43sec
   =5hr 64min 79sec
   79sec = 1min 19sec
   64min + 1 min = 65 min
   65min = 1hr 5 min
   5hr + 1hr = 6hr
   6hrs 5min 19 sec

4. C. 78.75km
   Solution:
   1hr 30min = 1.5 hr
   $25 \times 1.5 = 37.5$
   $27.5 \times 1.5 = 41.25$
   $37.5 + 41.25 = 78.75$

5. $\frac{3}{7}$
   Solution:
   $\frac{4+5}{4+5+12} = \frac{9}{21} = \frac{3}{7}$

6. D. 28°
   Solution:
   Let N be the 2nd angle
   1st angle = 2N+15
   3rd angle = 2N+15 + 10 = 2N+25
   2N+15 + N + 2N+25 = 180
   N = 28

7. 96 square meters
   Solution:
   L=3W-2
   P=2L+2W
   44=2(3W-2)+2W
   44=6W-4 + 2W
   W = 6
   L=3×6-2 = 16
   A = 16×6 = 96

8. 154 square meters
   Solution:
   $22/7 \times 7 \times 7 = 154$

9. A. £28
   Solution:
   $1+2+3+4+5+6+7 = 28$

10. $3\frac{61}{84}$ ft
    Solution:
    $5\frac{7}{12} - 1\frac{6}{7} = \frac{67}{12} - \frac{13}{7}$
    $\frac{469-156}{84} = \frac{313}{84} \ or \ 3\frac{61}{84}$

TEST 51 SOLUTION

1. C. 101250 ants
   Solution:
   1 month $=$ 4 weeks
   $1250 \times 3 \times 3 \times 3 \times 3 = 101250$

2. 1.48m
   Solution:
   4cm $=$ 0.04m
   20cm $=$ 0.2m
   $1.2 + 2 \times 0.04 + 0.2 = 1.48$

3. 5700 cm^3
   Solution:
   $300 \times 95\% \times 20 = 5700$

4. A. 323288 fried chickens
   Solution:
   2 weeks $=$ 14 days
   $11546 \times 14 \times 2 = 323288$

5. 392.4 Newtons
   Solution:
   $W = 9.81 \times m$
   $W = 9.81 \times 40 = 392.4$

6. C. £13300
   Solution:
   $\frac{4256}{8} \times 25 = 13300$

7. D. £5000
   Solution:
   $250 \div 5\% = 5000$

8. $\frac{1}{3}$
   Solution:
   $N + \frac{41}{5} = 8\frac{8}{15}$
   $N = \frac{128}{15} - \frac{41}{5}$
   $N = \frac{128}{15} - \frac{123}{15} = \frac{1}{3}$

9. A. 360 dm^3
   Solution:
   $V = 10 \times 12 \times 3 = 360$

10. $2 \times 2 \times 2 \times 3 \times 3 \times 5$
    Solution:
    $360 \div 2 = 180$
    $180 \div 2 = 90$
    $90 \div 2 = 45$
    $45 \div 3 = 15$
    $15 \div 3 = 5$
    $5 \div 5 = 1$
    $2 \times 2 \times 2 \times 3 \times 3 \times 5$

TEST 52 SOLUTION

1. 548 students
   Solution:

	Boys	Girls
Grade 1	34	72
Grade 2	65	61
Grade 3	43	55
Grade 4	54	63
Grade 5	26	75
Total	222	326

   Total: 222+326 = 548

2. A. 905 hollow blocks
   Solution:
   $72.4 \times 12.5 = 905$

3. £1248
   Solution:
   Discount $= 1560 \times 20\% = 312$
   $1560 - 312 = 1248$

4. B. 0.2475 m³
   Solution:
   V$=1.5 \times 0.55 \times 0.45 = 0.37125$
   $0.37125 \times \frac{1}{3} = 0.2475$

5. 125
   Solution:
   The pattern is n×n×n
   $1 \times 1 \times 1 = 1$
   $2 \times 2 \times 2 = 8$
   $3 \times 3 \times 3 = 27$
   $4 \times 4 \times 4 = 64$
   $5 \times 5 \times 5 = 125$

6. 3
   Solution:
   $(10\% \times 25\%) \times 8 \times 15$
   $0.025 \times 120 = 3$

7. C. 20 years old
   Solution:
   Brother's age today
   $2 \times 5 = 10$
   Brother's age after 10 years
   $10 + 10 = 20$

8. (-1, 0)
   Solution:
   (-2-2+3, 4-1-3)
   (-1, 0)

9. C. 252 cans
   Solution:
   $1260 \div 20 = 63$
   $63 \times 4 = 252$

10. B. 21 days
    Solution:
    $50 \times 25 = 1250$
    $26250 \div 1250 = 21$

TEST 53 SOLUTION

1. C. 180g
   Solution:
   $300×5\%×12 = 180$

2. 8 minutes
   Solution:
   $1.2÷9 = 0.133333$hrs
   0.13333hrs $× 60 = 8$minutes

3. B. 0.88m
   Solution:
   From XL to XS, it decreases 4 times
   $1.2-0.08×4 = 0.88$

4. 1455.75grams
   Solution:
   $50+125.75+80+1200 = 1455.75$

5. 782 platoon leaders
   Solution:
   $156400÷200 = 782$

6. 37800 cm³
   Solution:
   $200×3.15×60 = 37800$

7. B. 374 light bulbs
   Solution:
   $12:1 = 408:N$
   $N=34$
   $408-34 = 374$

8. A. $\frac{12}{131}$
   Solution:

	Smoking	On Drugs
Male	45	**12**
Female	20	54

   Total: $45+20+12+54 = 131$
   Male that is on drugs $= 12$
   $\frac{12}{131}$

9. 108^0
   Solution:

   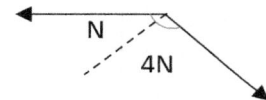

   $N+4N = 135$
   $5N=135$
   $N=27$
   $4N=108$

10. B. £109.7
    Solution:
    $120-7.5-2.8 = 109.7$

TEST 54 SOLUTION

1. 17 days
    Solution:
    $255 \div 15 = 17$

2. D. 11
    Solution:

    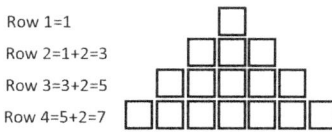
    Row 1=1
    Row 2=1+2=3
    Row 3=3+2=5
    Row 4=5+2=7

    Row 5=7+2=9
    Row 6=9+2=11

3. A. 4 ft
    Solution:
    1 foot = 12 inches
    48in $\div$ 12 = 4

4. D. 2 hours
    Solution:
    3days $\times$ 24 = 72hrs
    72-70 = 2

5. 200 bricks
    Solution:
    50kg=50000g
    50000$\div$250=200

6. 200 iPhones
    Solution:
    450-250 = 200

7. B. $3\frac{1}{6}$ kg
    Solution:
    $$8\frac{2}{3} - 5\frac{1}{2} = \frac{26}{3} - \frac{11}{2}$$
    $$\frac{52}{6} - \frac{33}{6} = \frac{19}{6} \; or \; 3\frac{1}{6}$$

8. 650,000

9. C. 168 marbles
    Solution:
    9.6-1.2 = 8.4kg
    8.4kg = 8400g
    8400$\div$50 = 168

10. 256 pages
    Solution:
    8$\times$32 = 256

TEST 55 SOLUTION

1. D. $\frac{19}{25}$

   Solution:

   $50-12 = 38$

   $\frac{38}{50} = \frac{19}{25}$

2. 86

   Solution:

   5 exam, median is the 3rd

   79,82,86,92,93

   3rd =86

3. 30 m²

   Solution:

   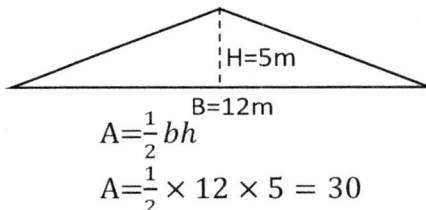

   $A=\frac{1}{2}bh$

   $A=\frac{1}{2} \times 12 \times 5 = 30$

4. B. 0.5m

   Solution:

   V=L×W×H

   6=4×3×H

   H=6÷12=0.5

5. Million

6. 2000g of eat

   Solution:

   Cat = 500

   Dog = 3×500 = 1500

   500+1500=2000

7. B. 1.48ºC

   Solution:

   45.12-43.64 = 1.48

8. C. £875

   Solution:

   $500 \times \frac{3}{4} = 375$

   500+375 = 875

9. A. 30

   Solution:

   No. of girls

   $90 \times \frac{1}{3} = 30$

   No. of boys

   90-30 = 60

   $60 \times \frac{3}{4} \times \frac{2}{3} = 30$

10. 17

    Solution:

    135-59 = 76

    76-59 = 17

Printed in Great Britain
by Amazon